# Globalization and Governance

To Jonathan, for opposing globalization, and to Miranda, for embracing it.

# Globalization and Governance

Jon Pierre

*Research Professor, Department of Political Science, University of Gothenburg, Sweden, and Adjunct Professor, University of Pittsburgh, USA and Nordland University, Bodö, Norway*

**Edward Elgar**

Cheltenham, UK • Northampton, MA, USA

Published by
Edward Elgar Publishing Limited
The Lypiatts
15 Lansdown Road
Cheltenham
Glos GL50 2JA
UK

Edward Elgar Publishing, Inc.
William Pratt House
9 Dewey Court
Northampton
Massachusetts 01060
USA

A catalogue record for this book
is available from the British Library

Library of Congress Control Number: 2013936172

This book is available electronically in the ElgarOnline.com
Social and Political Science Subject Collection, E-ISBN 978 1 78254 982 6

ISBN 978 1 84980 179 9 (cased)

Typeset by Servis Filmsetting Ltd, Stockport, Cheshire
Printed and bound in Great Britain by T.J. International Ltd, Padstow

# Contents

# Acknowledgements

Conducting a three-country comparative research project would not have been possible without the support of colleagues in the two countries I have been visiting. In Japan, Akira Nakamura and Masao Kikuchi at Meiji University have been a source of never-ending ideas for help and problem-solving while never losing their liberating sense of humor and self-distance. Akiko Takeoka and the rest of the staff at the Toshi Center—the Urban Center of Japan—were extremely professional and helpful in conducting the questionnaire study among Japanese local governments. The International House of Japan in Tokyo provided accommodation with characteristic seclusion in the heart of Tokyo.

This research has also benefited from the series of interviews I carried out for another project with the staff of the Osaka Prefectural Institute for Advanced Economic Development. Yoshiaki Jagouishi and Koji Shinjo, at different times Presidents of the Institute, have generously offered assistance. Takumi Hirai and Sawako Mauyama, at different times researchers at the Institute, have been extremely helpful in providing data on Japanese local and regional government, particularly on Osaka and the Kansai region. Toshio Kamo at Ritsumeikan University and Hiromi Tsuruta at Kansai University have generously offered their time to help me understand the complexities of inter-governmental relationships in Japan.

In Pittsburgh, for a long time my second academic home, Guy Peters and Matthew Weinstein were instrumental in getting the US questionnaire study organized and circulated. Guy's friendship and continuing support of the project has been integral to its completion. Also in Pittsburgh, Robert (Tony) Walters and Ron Linden have taught me much about globalization and governance over the years.

At home in Gothenburg, Malin Forsberg helped me get the datasets in order. Lennart J. Lundqvist offered a characteristic mixture of wisdom and good humor, and Mattias Ottervik generously shared his knowledge on Japan and data analysis. Many colleagues, too many to mention, have supported the project in any number of ways.

The bulk of the book was completed during a year as a visiting research fellow at the School of Social and Political Sciences, University of Melbourne. I am very much indebted to Scott Brenton, Ann Capling, Mark Considine, Michael Crozier, Robyn Eckerseley, Adrian Little, Kate MacDonald, and Aaron Martin for support, helpful comments, and good company.

In addition to these supportive colleagues, I must also thank a number of colleagues and friends for support along the way. Earl Fry, John Halligan, Don Kettl, Ellis Krauss, Michio Muramatsu, Robert Pekkanen, and Asbjörn Röiseland have generously offered support and help at various stages of the project.

Monika Djerf-Pierre continues to be my toughest critic and my most loyal supporter. The book is dedicated to our two children for sharing our geographical, intellectual, and emotional journey through life with us.

The project has enjoyed financial support from the Swedish Science Council and the Wenner-Green Foundation.

Jon Pierre
Gothenburg, March 2013

# 1. Globalization and the state

And as they went, Tigger told Roo (who wanted to know)
all about the things that Tiggers can do.
"Can they fly?", said Roo.
"Yes", said Tigger, "they're very good flyers,
Tiggers are. Strorny good flyers."
"Oo", said Roo. "Can they fly as good as Owl?"
"Yes", said Tigger. "Only they don't want to".
A.A. Milne (1928), *The House at Pooh Corner*

## THE ARGUMENT IN BRIEF

This book is focused on the processes through which global ideas and norms for domestic political and institutional change are inserted into domestic governance arrangements. The analysis seeks to enhance our knowledge about the specific processes through which globally transmitted ideas are adopted, deferred, or rejected in domestic policy and institutional choice. While there is an extensive literature on the wider theme of globalization and the state, we know rather little about these micro-foundations of globalization, that is, the causal mechanisms that shape the linkages between "the global" and "the domestic".

The empirical analysis covers three areas of political decision-making—economic governance, inter-governmental relationships, and administrative reform—in Japan, Sweden, and the United States. The three areas deal primarily with issues related to what Philip Cerny (1990) calls "the architecture of the politics", that is, institutional arrangements shaping domestic governance. Thus, this is not so much a study on globalization and domestic policy as an analysis of the impact of globalization on domestic governance.

The main argument coming out of this analysis is that the state retains significant control over its domestic governance even in the era of globalization. The study corroborates the findings of studies arguing that the state remains a significant source of political control, exercising autonomous choice on its domestic governance arrangements. The institutional changes in domestic governance that can be observed over the past 15–20 years are overwhelmingly driven by endogenous agents and are rarely outcomes of global pressures. Institutional changes related to international influences tend to be adaptations to globalization rather than the result of globalization in itself.

What explains this pattern which takes issue with a number of studies arguing that globalization causes significant decline in state strength and autonomy? Four related explanations stand out in particular. First, the globalization argument is too static and underestimates the learning and adaptive capability of the state. A large number of countries experienced severe shocks as international capital speculated aggressively against their currency. Today, governments have learned that in a globalized economy maintaining fiscal and budgetary discipline is essential to protect the domestic economy from overseas speculation. As a result, global pressures can be controlled and accommodated.

Second, governments address salient problems independently of, and frequently prior to, global pressures. Global ideas for domestic reform are not diffuse, normative notions about desirable changes in domestic governance but represent specific solutions to specific problems. Certainly there are examples of reform driven more by ideas and norms than by problems. For the most part, however, these global ideas target broader institutional issues such as inefficiency problems in the public sector, decentralization, deregulating markets, and competition in service delivery. A recurrent pattern in this book is that these issues had been addressed for considerable time before they were promoted by international organizations.

Third, the globalization argument ignores the diversity of national contexts. There is a vast heterogeneity among national contexts with regard to the normative orientation of their regime; their institutional integrity; their experience in living with external contingencies such as trade dependency; the structure of their economy; and the extent to which they are transmitters or receivers of the normative dimensions of globalization. Even the advanced industrialized democracies differ significantly in terms of their international exposure and the extent to which domestic governance arrangements and public policy are geared to compensate economic constituencies that are exposed to international competition. These variables contribute to explain the degree to which a country can, and chooses to, reject global pressures.

Finally, global ideas and recommendations for domestic reform may serve as catalysts of reform rather than being the chief sources of reform. Globalization interacts with domestic politics through complex, contextualized processes. These interactions include routine exchanges between transnational institutions and domestic structures as well as specific measures in response to short-term crises. Particularly in response to financial crises, international institutions like the World Bank and the International Monetary Fund offer aid and support conditioned on specific domestic reform. Given the critical context, governments have had little choice but to consent to the proposals.

Globalization has had its strongest influence on states during financial crises, which themselves often were triggered by the global financial system. Countries that experienced such crises during the 1980s and 1990s were often subjected to international pressures twice; first by global speculation against the domestic economy, and secondly by international financial institutions who conditioned their aid on domestic neo-liberal reform. There is also a more long-term impact of globalization on nation states which manifests itself in an anticipatory behavior; Governments refrain from macroeconomic policies which would jeopardize the balance of the economy and trigger global speculation on the domestic economy.

This introductory chapter will first rehearse the academic debate on globalization. Against that backdrop, the chapter defines the theme of the book and introduces the case countries and the areas of empirical investigation.

## GLOBALIZATION

We live in the era of globalization. The Internet allows us to retrieve information from any corner of the world in fractions of a second and to communicate instantly with people in any country. Capital, goods, services and people move across national borders with little or no delay. In the economy, we find evidence almost daily on the powerful transformation of domestic economies as private capital relocates industries, people and knowledge from one continent to another. The media and the travel industry reinforce the image of the world as shrinking; no place on the planet is out of reach, and no place is exempt from the pressures—and opportunities—of globalization.

All states are exposed to the economic and political pressures of globalization but some countries are more resilient to those pressures than others. While a number of studies report this pattern (see, for instance, Garrett, 1995; Swank, 2002; Wade, 1996), it seems to raise almost as many questions as it answers. To Sven Steinmo (2012), diversity itself is the key analytical puzzle and he applies an evolutionary model to explain how Japan, Sweden and the United States have evolved over an extended period of time. By observing these three countries as evolving systems, Steinmo shows how in each case adapting governance to an increasingly complex world, where globalization is only one of several sources of contingencies, is obstructed by institutional, political or cultural factors. Importing policies from overseas "creates friction between . . . political and social institutions" (Steinmo, 2012:231) in Japan and maintaining a universal welfare state in Sweden becomes a challenge in an increasingly heterogeneous society with low thresholds for foreign labor or refugees to enter the country. Thus, diversity in Steinmo's account is explained largely by the systems' limited capacity to adapt, or mistakenly adapting to what is believed to be emergent dominant norms.

Other scholars focus on the degree to which domestic institutional factors explain the variation in national sensitivity to globalization, or the configuration of the political economy, or the capacity of governments to harness the opportunities that globalization offers. Underlying much of this literature is an implicit assumption that adaptation to global neo-liberal norms and values is essential to future national competitiveness. National economies develop different instruments of coordination and resource allocation in order to foster international competitiveness (Hall and Soskice, 2001). Some countries place trust in the market to generate and reproduce a competitive business sector whereas other countries accord a role for government to regulate the market and to use various instruments to promote competitiveness.

Over time, the organization of state–market relations and the roles of the market and government become institutionalized in systems of national or regional political economies. For instance, it is intriguing to note the fundamental role which private financial institutions accord government even in the largely deregulated international financial markets (Helleiner, 1994; Mosley, 2003). To the business community, regulatory frameworks and state–market relations more widely become "rules of the game" (North, 1990) which help explain why German corporations behave differently from American or Argentinean corporations. They may all be players in international markets, and complex patterns of multinational ownership beg the question of how we define the nationality of a corporation. Even so, these key features of national political economy have proven resilient to the global economic forces, perhaps more so than most observers had expected.

As should already be obvious, understanding the drivers and consequences of globalization is a significant challenge. This is largely due to the complex and manifold nature of the phenomenon under study. Globalization is driven by technological development, by policy, and most of all by economic interests and changes in the regulatory frameworks of international capital. Together, these and other catalysts of globalization have transformed world politics and world trade from the end of the Second World War to the present date. Although this book will certainly consider the drivers of globalization, its main focus is on the domestic response to global signals for policy change. Strictly speaking this will not be a book about globalization per se but about the degree to which the trajectory of reform in three sectors of governance in three countries is shaped primarily by global forces or by domestic institutions. Thus, although set against the backdrop of global economic and political change, this will be a book about domestic politics; the politics and policies of domestic accommodation of global political and economic pressures through institutional or regulatory change or change of policy.

## The Globalization Debate

Few social science phenomena have been more extensively researched than globalization, yet it is difficult to find a research field with a more divided community of scholars than globalization. With regard to the impact of globalization on the nation state, some (e.g. Boyer and Drache, 1996; Mann, 1997; Pierre and Peters, 2000; Sörensen, 2004; Shaw, 1997) argue that globalization has propelled a transformation of the formal and effective capabilities of the state without necessarily reducing the governing capability of the state whereas others (see, for instance, Camilleri and Falk, 1992; Ohmae, 1995; Strange, 1996) maintain that globalization has meant a significant weakening of the state.

Perhaps the most powerful argument on this issue has been delivered by Linda Weiss (Weiss, 1998, 1999, 2000): "The dispute between globalists and skeptics is *not* about the *reality* of change; it is about the nature and significance of the changes under way as well as the forces behind them", she argues (Weiss, 1999:59; original italics). For Weiss and several other scholars in this debate, the key point is thus not globalization per se but rather the degree to which it has impacted the governing capacity of the state.[1] This perspective thus defines globalization and domestic institutional resilience as interdependent and contextualized phenomena where the issue is not so much the "absolute" force of globalization but primarily the "net" balance between that force and the resilience of domestic institutions. There is no categorical and definitive answer to the question to what extent globalization has weakened the governing capacity of the state.

Advocates of globalization maintain that as far as economic growth goes increasing international trade and the removal of trade barriers lead to a more efficient allocation of natural and other resources. A major argument supporting globalization is thus its integrative dimension; global mobility of goods and people will create more efficient markets than the current which in many cases still suffer from national tariffs to protect domestic interests. Globalization, the advocate further argue, will create a more efficient "spatial division of labor" (see Massey, 1995) where the location of value-added processes and production is guided by the market and not the outcome of political processes. This emergent global division of labor and the opening up of markets and increasing mobility of goods and people will bring prosperity to all.

The globalization protagonists also suggest that free markets and mobility of production factors will induce locales (cities, regions, countries) to develop a competitive niche within global competition (compare with Ohmae, 1995). Nation states were integral to the consolidation of political democracy and the rule of law but in the early third millennium they have lost much of their *raison d'être* as an organizing paradigm of politics, the economy, and social life. In terms of the diffusion of information, increasing travel and global "connectedness" are also important components of the integrative aspect of globalization. Thus, in the eyes of the globalization advocates, globalization represents the liberalization of markets and business, free and instant communication, and a dismantling of domestic structures which may have played a historical role in securing democratic governance and basic social welfare, but which now, like the Twelve Apostles—a line of limestone stacks just off the Australian south coast between Princetown and Peterborough—merely indicate a demarcation of some previous historical significance.

At the other side of the controversy, critics, or "skeptics", of globalization rarely question the integrative aspects of this profound development. Instead they take issue with what they see as the normative foundation and discourse of globalization. They see globalization as a project driven by corporate and economic interests aiming at dismantling domestic regulatory frameworks of capital and markets, cutting taxes, deregulating labor markets, and opening up domestic markets to overseas companies. They also point out that globalization exacerbates global economic inequalities and places markets over politics, thereby depriving the citizens of the countries of the world perhaps their only lever to articulate and pursue collective interests: collective action and political control (Amoore et al., 1997; Boyer and Drache, 1996; Camilleri and Falk, 1992; Mann, 1997; Weiss, 1999).

Globalization "skeptics" furthermore criticize the powerful neo-liberal discourse of globalization and its tendency to subtly but firmly impose Western neo-liberal values on governments across the world. If policy makers are led to believe that extensive deregulation and tax cuts are essential in order for the country to remain competitive in the globalized economy, then that is the agenda they will pursue. They will also be convinced that since investment capital is now deregulated, global and basically foot-loose, it is integral to national prosperity that public policy does not run against corporate interests as this would trigger a massive exodus of private capital (Hay and Rosamond, 2002; Hirst and Thompson, 1999).

"Skeptics" also criticize globalization as they see it as a threat to the nation state and thus to the big political projects implemented by the state such as democracy and social welfare. Not least for these reasons, globalization is a politically highly charged phenomenon. Few will take issue with the technological revolution and the unprecedented access to information worldwide. Instead it is the purported global inequalities that globalization entails and the weakening of domestic institutions that have driven the critique against globalization (see Stiglitz, 2003).

Many of the globalization "skeptics" have focused their criticism on the close linkage between the discourse of globalization and neo-liberal economic policy. Linda Weiss suggests that the domestic policy change towards neo-liberal policies in the advanced democracies has to a significant extent been driven not by powerful manifestations of global economic pressures but by a belief among policy makers that such pressures exist and that policy therefore must change to help ensure that the domestic economy remains competitive in this changing global economy. States still control powerful levers to control the domestic economy but choose not to use those levers as the globalization discourse argues that it would be detrimental to the economy in the new, globalized landscape. Globalization, Weiss points out, became the political pretext for many governments to implement a neo-liberal agenda (Weiss, 1998; see also Hay and Rosamond, 2002; Steinmo, 2012), and like Tigger's colorful account in the opening of this chapter of what his species is capable of doing, states still have the capacity to regulate the economy but choose not to.

This close linkage between globalization and a neo-liberal domestic policy agenda has been sustained by a discourse emphasizing that in a globalized world the primacy of the market is stronger than perhaps ever before. Equally important, this discourse will hold that policy choice is no longer controlled by domestic institutions; even if a strong political majority take issue with the neo-liberal agenda, economic realities would prevent that—or if they did it would seriously jeopardize the country's competitiveness and prosperity (Weiss, 1998). The fundamental normative elements of the neo-liberal globalization discourse defined a new role for the state and market not just in economic policy but in administrative reform as well (Suleiman, 2003).

However, as Beeson and Capling (2002:295) remind us, "discourse is a necessary but not sufficient engine of change". Translating discourse into public policy requires agency; politicians who articulate the values and objectives of the discourse and put forth proposals on the political agenda towards those objectives. The neo-liberal globalization discourse provided support to political parties of that ideological orientation. However, it confronted all political players with the same basic challenge; if the country is to remain competitive it has little choice but to follow suit with the United States and the UK and deregulate its financial markets and implement an economic policy that will attract global investment.

The persuasive force of this argument cannot be exaggerated. In addition, for many countries in Europe the globalization argument dovetailed with the requirements related to the continuing integration in the EU. In Sweden, the Social Democratic government in 1989 went ahead and deregulated the currency market following a decision-making process that lacked political conviction as much as it lacked stringent analysis of the ramifications of such a deregulation. Instead, the driving arguments to deregulate the markets were that most of Sweden's competitors had already deregulated their financial markets and Sweden could not afford to lose competitiveness, and also that deregulation would increase the efficiency of the market (see Telasuo, 2000:162–4). Combined with a bubble economy in its real estate market and a national budget rapidly generating deficits, the deregulation of the currency market and other financial markets was a key trigger of the 1992 financial crisis in Sweden (Pierre, 1999; Telasuo, 2000). Thus, the globalization discourse, translated into the necessities of EU integration, national competitiveness and market efficiency, confronted all significant players with a policy prescription which was very difficult to resist, particularly as the deregulation bandwagon gained momentum in the Western world.

It is intriguing to note the strength of the globalization argument on public policy, primarily economic policy, when considering the significant uncertainty about what globalization and its challenges to the state actually meant. Few political players were willing to challenge the globalization argument although its validity had yet to be proven. What would happen to a country that chose not to deregulate financial and other domestic markets, cut back in public expenditure and cut taxes? No one had the answer to this question but neither was anyone willing to gamble on the future prosperity of the country. Political parties on the right end of the ideological spectrum used the globalization argument to sustain its policies while leftist parties struggled to present an alternative response to the thesis.

## THE AMERICAN CENTURY?

The era of globalization is embedded in what has been referred to as "the American century" (Eckes and Zeiler, 2003). Norms of free trade, liberalization of markets, and limited government which are at the core of the globalization argument are the norms that the American government has been trying to convey to other countries throughout the twentieth century. From a distinctly American perspective Eckes and Zeiler (2003:238) suggest that "the defining theme of the post-Cold War era—and indeed of the entire American century—has been globalization". For these observers, the twentieth century saw an unprecedented expansion not only of US influence on the rest of the world in terms of goods, consumerism, and (after the fall of the Berlin Wall) political allegiances, but also in terms of culture and lifestyle. In a tenor not usually found in the scholarly literature, Eckes and Zeiler argue that after the devastations of the Second World War American businesses had a unique opportunity to sell almost anything to almost anyone: "Aware that a troubled world had an insatiable appetite for American values, goods and services, US leaders exploited their comparative advantage in communications and marketing to spread the American dream of democracy, prosperity, mass consumption, and individual enterprise. In the long Cold War, that formula proved a winner" (Eckes and Zeiler, 2003:131).

Nationalistic overtones aside, Eckes and Zeiler's account of "the American century" makes a crucial point about globalization which we will be returning to several times throughout the book; the notion that globalization in many observers' views spells Americanization. Thus, globalization, according to these critics, is less a process of dismantling nation–state barriers to trade or the flow of information across jurisdictional borders but more a matter of disseminating American economic, political and cultural values across the world (see, e.g. Altman, 2009a, 2009b). When French intellectuals bemoan *mondialisation*, most of them are probably more concerned about the import of US culture and politics to France than about the trade liberalization per se (Blyth, 2008:133); as legendary automobile maker Louis Renault once remarked, "if Ford and General Motors dominate the French markets, one and a half million Frenchmen will have died in vain in the last war" (quoted in Eckes and Zeiler, 2003:97). Similarly, when the Japanese could not tell US demands for market liberalization from the stern advice they received from the IMF and the World Bank as they tried to address a severe financial crisis in the late 1980s and 1990s, globalization easily translated into Americanization or "Westernization" (Itoh, 1998; Stronach, 1995).

Thus, what is at stake is perhaps not so much the boost of the capitalist economy which was the purported result of trade liberalization but rather the imposition of the culture and social norms, particularly American or Western norms, and the potential loss of national identity that followed suit (see Norris and Inglehart, 2009). In the mid-1990s, Susan Berger predicted that "the future of convergence is likely to be shaped by growing political opposition to changes that are perceived to be the response to external pressures" (Berger, 1996:23). The concrete manifestation of such opposition can obviously take many different forms, ranging from reluctance among the political and administrative elite of a country to implement policies which they believe are at odds with the policy style of the country to more widespread opposition against transnational organizations or "the West" and the values it represents.

Countries differ greatly with respect to the degree that they are primarily transmitters or receivers of the norms and policy prescriptions that globalization entails, and these differences play a major role in explaining the amount of change that countries have had to go through to adapt to globalization. These pressures for change have sometimes been defined less by nation states but more by transnational institutions like the International Monetary Fund (IMF), the World Bank, the World Trade Organization (WTO), and the Organisation for Economic Co-operation and Development (OECD). Even so, however, the policy recommendations issued by these institutions have tended to echo the interests of the US and the West more broadly. This does not mean that the US is not an interesting case to study in the context of globalization—opening up to global markets has in many ways been just as challenging to the US economy as it has to most other countries in terms of the structural changes it has triggered—but it does suggest that countries exporting the norms and values associated with a free, global economy have less adaptation to go through compared to countries with a history of a tighter regulatory grip on their economy.

The similarity between US political and economic interests and the recommendations issued by the IMF, the World Bank, and the Inter-American Development Bank is the essence of the

"Washington Consensus" argument, according to which these transnational institutions—all with their headquarters in Washington, DC—urge governments around the world to implement reform which conform to US corporate or political interests. From the point of view of the targeted country, it becomes virtually impossible to tell whether such recommendations originate from the US or the IMF or the World Bank as they tend to sound more or less alike (see Jayasuria, 2002; Philippi, 2003; Serra and Stiglitz, 2008; Stiglitz, 2003). Coined in 1990 by John Williamson, the "Washington Consensus" concept was originally "intended to identify those policies that mainstream Washington institutions like the US Treasury, the International Monetary Fund, the World Bank, and the Inter-American Development Bank agreed to be key to the restoration of growth in Latin America" (Kuczynski, 2003:24). Later, as the IMF and the World Bank took a more explicit neo-liberal stance in their recommendations, the "Washington Consensus" gradually evolved into referring to policies of deregulation, privatization, tax cuts, and cutbacks in the public budget.

Many observers, particularly neo-Marxist scholars (see for instance Nederveen Pieterse, 2004), have noted the synchronicity during the twentieth century between the rapid expansion of the US economy, the penetration of US companies in European, Asian and Latin American markets, the emerging American military predominance, and the increasing salience of the neo-liberal agenda that has defined much of US economic policy, not least since 1980. However, mainstream political science and international relations, too, have recorded this pattern (see Ikenberry, 2007). The US' ascendancy to global dominance began during the Cold War and accelerated after the fall of the Berlin Wall.

## TOWARD EMPIRICAL INQUIRY

Given the scope and range of globalization across all sectors of society, offering a comprehensive account of all aspects of globalization is a futile academic enterprise. As the impressive host of literature on the topic substantiates, there is an almost infinite range of approaches to globalization. It goes without saying that this strategy to get a grip on globalization leaves out much of what other observers believe to be perhaps the most significant aspects of globalization. Observers from academic fields such as economics, cultural studies, mass communication, anthropology, and international relations place almost completely different meanings into the concept of globalization. It is indicative that a keyword search for "globalization" at a good university library yields more than 5000 hits.

Even within the political science literature we find an almost endless line of studies on globalization, either using globalization as a cluster of explanatory variables (e.g. "globalization and the state") or seeking to explain some aspect of globalization. Furthermore, while there is now an extensive literature presenting macro-level analyses of countries' political and economic performance during globalization, we know less about how the influence of overseas ideas and agents on domestic political decision-making actually plays out.

Perhaps the biggest challenge in studying globalization is to delineate the study and to focus on a limited set of specific issues and a limited number of cases. True, there is much merit in the many previous large-N studies of the relationship between globalization and domestic policies or institutional arrangements (see, for instance, Swank, 2002). For the present study, however, it is essential that the research design targets a very limited set of issues and cases in order to allow for more in-depth analysis on the process through which international norms, ideas and programs are adopted in domestic policies.

Thus, while the big picture is relatively clear—keeping in mind the different perspectives on globalization discussed earlier—we still lack insight into the causal mechanisms of globalization. We know very little about the micro-foundations of globalization, that is, the context and process through which transnational norms are integrated (or "translated") into domestic policy and regulation. Why is it that national governments elect to change governance arrangements to accommodate ideas and concepts related to globalization? How is the necessity of such reform perceived; that is, how are global pressures for reform translated into domestic policy change? How are those new policies integrated with previous policies and what political and institutional issues arise as a consequence of such adoption of overseas policies? These are the question this book addresses. Our objective is not to explain what drives globalization or its consequences on a grand societal scale. Instead we are concerned with the relationship between globalization and domestic governance.

In order to uncover these micro-foundations of globalization, it is imperative to focus on a very limited number of empirical issues and an equally limited number of cases. The book studies processes of accommodation and change in response to global pressures in economic governance, administrative reform, and inter-governmental relationships in Japan, Sweden, and the United States. Throughout this analysis we assess the degree to which observed changes should be seen as responses to global or international forces, or whether they are mainly consistent with the path-dependent trajectory of reform typical to the country and sector in question. All areas of reform in all countries display some degree of change when observed over a longer period of time. Our challenge is to see to what extent globalization has led to a change of course in reform and, if possible, to assign causality to those developments.

This task is complicated by several theoretical and methodological circumstances. First, different countries facing similar environmental or demographic or economic challenges may implement similar policies or programs not so much because of international pressures but rather because of the similarity in terms of the challenges they face, for example in terms of demographic or social or economic developments (see Bennett, 1991; Boyer, 1996; Drezner, 2001; Lundqvist, 2012; Lynn, 2001; Pollitt, 2001, 2002). This means that convergence, which sometimes is seen as the ultimate proof of the power of globalization (Berger, 1996), may occur for a variety of reasons, only one of which is global political or economic pressures on domestic institutions.

To be sure, using convergence as an indicator of domestic sensitivity to global norms and economic pressures may be barking up the wrong tree altogether, partly because convergence can be the outcome of other processes than globalization and partly because national political economies can make adjustments in their governance and regulation which do not necessarily increase their similarity with the political economy of other countries.[2] As Steinmo shows, traditional welfare states face different challenges and therefore respond differently to globalization compared to Anglo-American or Asian states (Steinmo, 2012). One could, of course, argue that in a free market economy countries would adopt features of the political economy of their competitors (see Kester, 1996; Kosai, 1996) but that might be underestimating the institutionalization of foundational features of national economies. After all, there is a reason why different models of capitalism remain even after a couple of decades of a globalized economy (Hall and Soskice, 2001).

A second challenge is that public records, documents, and interviews may provide the public justification for domestic choice rather than the real underlying motives for such choice. The key decisions on how to design reform and the role of international ideas and norms in that process are extremely difficult to uncover by an external observer.

We will now briefly introduce the three areas of reform and the three countries under study. Chapter 2 will present an overarching analysis of different types of global pressures on the state and different strategies of accommodation as a response to those pressures. Then Chapters 3–5 are devoted to analyses of economic governance, inter-governmental relationships and administrative reform. Chapter 6 offers some conclusions on domestic governance in a globalizing world.

## THREE REFORM SECTORS: ECONOMIC GOVERNANCE, INTER-GOVERNMENTAL RELATIONSHIPS, AND ADMINISTRATIVE REFORM

As already mentioned, the key focus of the present analysis is not on substantive policy sectors but on governance, more specifically to what degree and through which processes globalization changes domestic governance, domestic institutional arrangements and the role of those institutions.[3] Kanishka Jayasuria argues that "globalisation brings with it a new ensemble of governance institutions, and it is these new structures that shape and influence the architecture of domestic states. Thus globalisation changes the internal architecture of the state" (Jayasuria, 2002:28). We are interested in testing Jayasuria's hypothesis by identifying the drivers of institutional change and the degree to which global ideas have driven such change.

The study is concentrated on three areas of domestic governance; changes in the regulatory framework of domestic markets, inter-governmental relationships, and administrative reform. These three sectors capture different aspects of the organization of domestic governance. Thus we are not studying sectors of public policy; our focus is on to what extent and through which channels globalization has reshaped domestic governance. Governance arrangements may certainly have an indirect effect on policy insofar as they represent different institutional arrangements and different models of public authority in those arrangements (Weaver and Rockman, 1993).

## Economic Governance

The first aspect of domestic governance is market regulation and the presence of government in the market more broadly. Governments in all countries exercise more or less regulatory control over domestic markets to coordinate the economy, support national competitiveness, and protect public interests and consumer interests. The extent and purpose of political presence in the market varies considerably across time and space. Extensive research on comparative political economy shows the existence of two different models, or what Albert (1993:5) calls "two divergent currents, two broad 'schools'", of capitalism; the Anglo-American "liberal market economy" on the one hand, and the "Rhineland" (Albert, 1993) or "coordinated market economy" on the other (Hall and Soskice, 2001).

These two models of a capitalist economy essentially define different roles for the state in the economy. They represent different institutional arrangements which have evolved over considerable time (Hall, 1986; Hall and Soskice, 2001; North, 1990), defining roles for the political sphere and for market actors towards promoting economic growth and international competitiveness. An important element of the institutionalization of the models is that they define mutual expectations on roles and behavior on both sides of the border between the public and the private spheres of society. Japanese businesses have different expectations on government—and vice versa—than American businesses but in both cases the roles of public and private agents are believed to be optimal to promote national competitiveness.

This aspect of domestic governance has been a key feature of the globalization debate. Globalization (so far) is primarily an economic phenomenon, and the tenor of the economic imperative of globalization is the promotion of a neo-liberal economic model of capitalism. The basic philosophy of economic globalization is that economic efficiency and national competitiveness in the deregulated economic landscape does not stem from the state coordinating market actors but rather from the competiveness of individual firms and the capacity of the state to attract global investment capital. Both of these sources of competitiveness are predicated on a relaxation of domestic regulatory frameworks coupled with low taxes and cuts in public expenditure.

In this theme we are thus interested in how national governments have responded to transnational pressures to reorganize their economic governance. What has been the source of such pressures; what specific elements of economic governance has been the target of those pressures; and how have national governments related their economic policies and governance to those pressures?

## Inter-governmental Relationships

The second analytical theme in this study is to what extent globalization has impacted the relationship between central, regional and local government. These institutional arrangements are obviously integral to domestic governance, yet it might not be obvious how they speak to the present issues. Why would we expect such institutional change to be driven by globalization? Why is the study of subnational government relevant to an analysis of globalization and domestic governance? What are the causal linkages between globalization, inter-governmental relationships and urban and regional politics?

There are several reasons why inter-governmental relationships are an area worthy of analysis in the present context. During the late 1980s and 1990s, globalization, coupled with a neo-liberal regime that allowed for uneven economic development among cities and regions, has profoundly challenged subnational government (Parkinson and Judd, 1988; Storper and Walker, 1989). As globalization has matured and its impact on states, regions, and cities has become increasingly articulated, its impact has in many ways been stronger and more direct on subnational economies and institutions than on national political economies.

Globalization has also been found to have a stronger impact on subnational government because that is where dominant features of globalization like migration, urbanization and global economic competition are most strongly felt. It is at the level of local and regional government that some accommodation of migration and unemployment is required (Hambleton and Simone Gross, 2007). Central government is assumed to mitigate the impact of globalization on subnational government (Beauregard, 1995), and state institutions traditionally assist subnational government in accommodating migration. That having been said, however, the organizational challenge is found at the regional and local levels of the political system.

Moreover, globalization and internationalization has coincided with, and frequently driven, important processes of domestic institutional change. Nation–state economic policies in the advanced Western democracies during the 1980s and 1990s have increasingly emphasized neo-liberal goals such as tax cuts, deregulation and cutbacks in the public sector. Those policies tend to leave cities and regions less protected from international political and economic pressures, compared to the previously dominant policy style of higher taxes, more regulation, a more resource-full and intervening public sector. Subsidies from central to subnational government were previously more common and generous than they tend to be today and worked both as a means of steering but also to compensate cities and regions for implementing national policy. While subsidies are still transferred it is fair to say that subnational governments in most countries are today more self-reliant than they were a few decades ago. The combined effect of neo-liberal policies at the central government level and decreasing subsidies from central to subnational government has been that many cities and regions have begun to explore other sources of revenues and economic development, including overseas networks (see Chapter 4).

Another domestic institutional change which has been driven by international contingencies (at least in Europe) is related to the continuing integration and consolidation of the European Union. The EU evolved as a "Europe of the Regions" (Le Galès and Lequesne, 1998) and targeted regions more than the member states for its structural funds. This policy design prompted member states to strengthen the regional level so that regions would be eligible and competitive for EU funds (Smyrl, 1997). Regional policy has been an important driver of multi-level governance in the EU where transnational institutions engage cities or regions—and vice versa—while by-passing the level of member state governments (Bache and Flinders, 2004; Hooghe and Marks, 2003; Marks et al., 1996; Newman, 2000; Piattoni, 2010).

Together these developments have redefined relationships between states, regions and cities. Neil Brenner describes these changes as a "rescaling" whereby the previous hierarchical institutional order is replaced by a more complex arrangement which allows subnational governments to pursue their interests in a wider set of arenas, more or less independently of the state. Brenner, echoing Jayasuria (2002) sees such a breakup of domestic institutional hierarchies as linked to globalization (see Brenner 1999, 2004; van der Heiden, 2010).

To sum up, there are plenty of reasons to investigate the impact of globalization on domestic institutional arrangements. Institutional change in the era of globalization has not so much been aimed at providing shelter or "cushions" for subnational government as it is exposed to global pressures for adjustment. Instead, it has been a strategy to reconfigure the state to make the country as a whole competitive in international arenas and markets. To what extent have cities and regions embarked on international strategies in the era of globalization? How has national policy towards subnational government changed during globalization?

## Administrative Reform

The 1980s, 1990s and 2000s so far have not only been the era of globalization. This is also the time period of extensive public sector reform aimed at modernizing public administration and public service delivery. Such reform was not an entirely new idea. What differed from previous reform efforts this time was that reform aimed not just at issues of lacking efficiency and flexibility in the public sector but also the fundamental normative framework of public administration and the degree to which public administration is different from private sector service delivery (Christensen and Laegreid, 2011; Peters, 2001; Pierre, 2011a; Pollitt and Bouckaert, 2011). In particular, the "New Public Management" (NPM) reform strategy aimed at bringing the market and private sector management models into the public sector.

NPM emerged in the UK but was soon picked up by the World Bank and the OECD and was promoted as a program of public sector reform in member states and loan takers. The OECD created a section, PUMA, devoted to promoting public management reform in its member states, and the World Bank and the IMF conditioned loans and other forms of support on deregulation, privatization and other NPM measures (see for instance Turner, 2002). At this stage, NPM reform was implemented or considered by the vast majority of countries in the world, and its ideas of what the future public administration would look like were debated in Tokyo, Montevideo, Rome, and Canberra. It appeared as if differences in what specific problems the bureaucracy in any of these capitals was facing or indeed differences in institutional arrangements, political and administrative culture and tradition carried little weight in the promotion of NPM. Unlike most other administrative reform campaigns, NPM was value-driven, not problem-driven (Suleiman, 2003) and national features were therefore not considered in the global diffusion of the reform model.

NPM, or market-based administrative reform more broadly, was implemented most extensively and swiftly in the Anglo-American democracies; first the UK, then Canada, New Zealand and Australia.[4] Guy Peters argues that NPM fits much better with the Anglo-American system of administration than the European or Asian systems which are based more in rules and legality than management and efficiency (Peters, 2001). Despite these important contextual differences, however, NPM has also been implemented in the Weberian *Reechtsstaat* systems of administration, albeit less extensively than in countries like New Zealand or the UK.

Thus here is another area of extensive state reform and the task before us is to investigate to what extent and through which types of processes this reform can be related to globalization or internationalization. It is correct, as Kettl (1997) argues, to describe this reform as a "global revolution in public management" but that is not the same as saying that administrative reform has been driven by globalization. It could just as well be a manifestation of similar problems of rising costs and frustrated clients in a wider variety of countries. How did the basic features of NPM relate to entrenched normative aspects of public administration? Through which channels were NPM brought into domestic contexts of administrative reform?

## THREE NATIONAL CONTEXTS: JAPAN, SWEDEN AND THE UNITED STATES

Japan, Sweden, and the United States tell rather different stories about how globalization has impacted their domestic governance.[5]

They all belong to the group of affluent industrial democracies that have increased their economic integration for the past century or so but most markedly since 1960. Japan built much of its spectacular economic recovery in the 1960s and 1970s on export revenues, acquiring technology from the West at moderate cost and excelling in the marketing of its consumer products in American and European markets (Johnson, 1982). Sweden, with its combination of a relatively speaking big industrial sector and a small domestic market had little choice but to explore overseas markets in order to facilitate an economy of scale for its industry. And the United States, finally, saw its growing industrial sector penetrating overseas markets with consumer goods and industrial products in the early decades of the twentieth century and well into the post-Second World War period (Eckes and Zeiler, 2003; Spulber, 1995). Thus, the Americans, Japanese and Swedes were very familiar with the complex contingencies and challenges that come with trade dependency long before the globalization era of the 1980s onwards. Their strategies to tackle those contingencies differed, however, as we will see later.

The three countries also differ in many key aspects. The most conspicuous difference is obviously size; Japan with a population of some 127 million, Sweden with just less than 10 million, and the US with about 314 million. The emergent US industry in the nineteenth century had a huge domestic market to saturate before it would have to consider foreign market ventures. Sweden, by contrast, had little to offer in terms of domestic market demand. Japan falls between these two extremes; the domestic market was for a long time sufficiently strong to sustain a sizeable manufacturing industry—although the financial crisis of the 1990s effectively curtailed domestic demand—but a more long-term objective of Japanese economic development is related to national security and independence. The close relationship between such core national values and economic growth helps understand the dynamics of the tripod of business, bureaucracy, and senior politicians that governed the Japanese economy during its renowned "economic miracle" during the 1960s and 1970s (Johnson, 1982; Okimoto, 1988).

The size and buoyancy but also the governance of domestic markets is integral to an understanding of the pressures that global economic forces can throw at a national economy. Government obviously has much less problems controlling the domestic market than overseas trade fluctuations; macroeconomic policy can stimulate domestic demand, control inflation, and curb unemployment, and so on. International trade, on the other hand, is virtually impossible to control for any individual country and here we see bigger differences between the three countries. Trade in Japan and the United States since the mid-1980s accounts for about 20 percent of the GDP, to be compared with 60 percent or more in Sweden (see Figure 1.1). Indeed, in 2008 Sweden was one of rather few countries to have its trade exceed 100 percent of GDP (see Garrett and Mitchell, 2001; OECD Statistics).

These trade data would suggest that Sweden, along with other high-trade countries like Belgium and the Netherlands, is more vulnerable to fluctuations in the global economy and to changes in the strategy of global investment capital than are the United States or Japan. But Sweden has developed political and economic mechanisms to cushion the impact of internationalization. The welfare state, which many observers saw as basically incompatible with a globalized economy, has proven resilient, and, indeed, "increasing welfare state effort mitigates these [globalization] pressures and hence helps maintain public support for openness . . . the stability generated by the welfare state has direct benefits for investment, productivity, growth and competitiveness" (Garrett and Mitchell, 2001:152; see also Katzenstein, 1984; Korpi, 2003).

As these brief introductory observations on the US, Japan and Sweden in the globalization era suggest, economic factors are important but they do not determine the impact of globalization or the domestic accommodation of global pressures. Thus, as Garrett and Mitchell (2001) convincingly show, high levels of foreign direct investment do *not* dictate governments to cut taxes; capital mobility has *not* forced welfare states to embark on a race to the bottom; and high levels of capital mobility have *not* stopped some governments from insisting on progressive forms of taxation. The puzzle is much more complicated and dynamic than the basic globalization argument stipulates. To understand how globalization impacts a country we must look both at the nature of global pressures—their sources, the processes through which they are conveyed, and so on—as well as the governing capacity of the state and the degree to which globalization corresponds with domestic policy preferences. The strength of globalization can only be understood from the interaction between the global and the domestic (Weiss, 1998).

The expansion of international trade and deregulation of financial markets have presented governments and industry with a set of powerful challenges, but several circumstances contribute to mitigating those pressures; domestic institutions, domestic constituencies protecting welfare state programs, and policy compensating domestic actors exposed to globalization. The uniform, global race to the bottom which some observers saw as an inevitable (in some cases desirable) consequence of economic globalization has not happened. Domestic factors such as institutional arrangements, public policy, organized interests and political agency all contribute to translating transnational signals for change into domestic programs which can be implemented within the long-term trajectory of a country's development (see Steinmo, 2012).

Let us now look somewhat more closely at how the three countries have related to globalization more broadly. We will obviously discuss these issues in greater detail later in the book.

## Japan

Japan presents an intriguing, almost paradoxical image of globalization. While all industrialized democracies have been exposed to global political and economic pressures, urging some form of domestic response or accommodation, "none seems more challenged by these pressures than Japan, a country that has resisted global rules for its domestic markets for many years", argue Schaede and Grimes (2003a:xi). The post-war period saw Japan emerging as an economic superpower, successfully penetrating overseas markets with highly competitive products. This unparalleled case of economic recovery and development—the renowned "Japanese miracle"—was facilitated by a combination of a domestic economic and industrial organization creating optimal conditions for industrial expansion and productivity, the acquisition of technologies developed overseas, and the insulation of domestic markets.

At the same time, the Japanese mentality of *sakoku* ("secluded nation") provided and justified economic and social barriers against similar encroachment of Japan's domestic markets. The Japanese make a useful distinction between inward and outward globalization. Several observers note a profound tension in Japanese culture between s*akoku* and *kokusaika* (internationalization), even suggesting that *kokusaika* "has been a mere coerced Westernization" (Itoh,

1998:13; also, see Stronach, 1995). Itoh (1998) notes that while Japan has excelled in outward *kokusaika*, primarily in economic terms, it has failed to elevate its political significance in world affairs to the same level as its economic standing. And, it has not succeeded in inward *kokusaika*; the Japanese society has not embraced overseas cultures and values and when such values have been adopted it has been incrementally and reluctantly (see Vinh, 2004).

This argument obviously deserves further elaboration and we will return to the issue of the extent to which Japan has adopted norms, values, and institutional models from overseas. The Japanese seem to make a careful distinction between concepts of reform that they themselves detect overseas and voluntarily incorporate into the Japanese state—as was for instance the case during the Meiji restoration in 1868 (see Chapter 5)—on the one hand, and reform concepts which they see as imposed on them on the other.

For the present analysis it is analytically important to differentiate between pressures of globalization and the type of domestic adaptation to trade conditions that all industrial democracies face. From the vantage point of the individual country, however, differences between bilateral pressures or global pressures or pressures from international financial institutions are academic; they all require some strategy of accommodation or adaptation. This perspective is central to the debate concerning the Washington Consensus where targeted countries could not distinguish between bilateral or multilateral pressures on domestic choice. For instance, the "trade friction" issues between the United States and Japan in the 1980s were a bilateral exchange that initially had little to do with globalization but later became part of the negotiations between international institutions and the Japanese government (see Chapter 3).

### Sweden

Sweden's experience with globalization has some commonalities with Japan but it also differs in many respects. Sweden remains deeply dependent on export revenues, as we have seen. A growing concern has been that a large part of those revenues still come from a very limited number of big companies with a long experience in operating in overseas markets. It has for long been a lingering problem that these internationally successful players all tend to be mature companies in potentially declining markets, like the automobile companies Volvo and Saab or the ball-bearing manufacturer SKF. True, among these international corporations we also find Sony Ericsson and several companies in the research-intensive medical sector.

However, for the large number of small and medium-sized businesses, pursuing export ventures is still off the agenda. Government offers incentives, institutional support, and even some socialization of risk for companies who decide to explore international markets. Even so, the number of small and medium-sized companies who decide to take that step has remained steady at just above 10 percent since the early 2000s (Tillväxtverket, 2012). Thus, the structure of the business community delivering Sweden's export revenues is concentrated around a very limited number of corporations with uncertain growth potential.

Economic governance in the post-war period has been characterized by this rather unusual economic configuration. Income taxes have been high by any international comparison, but so have the social benefits and support programs. Labor market policies have aimed at facilitating structural change in the economy, triggered by changes in the international markets and changing factor costs which redefine the comparative advantage of the Swedish economy. Throughout the post-war period Sweden has been a high-income, high-tax society with its key corporate structures involved in competition in international markets; a seemingly impossible equation. The solution has been to keep corporate taxes low; to accommodate and retrain laid-off labor; to prioritize the knowledge- and research-intensive end of the economy; and to provide institutional and political stability. In a word, Sweden chose the path-dependent high-road approach to accommodate its international contingencies and stood relatively well prepared for the more powerful, deregulated global economy as it evolved in the 1980s and 1990s (see Lindbeck, 1998; Sölvell and Porter, 1993).[6]

Alongside this hierarchical business community and the peculiar type of economic governance which is typical to a small, trade-dependent country sits a public sector which is customarily referred to as the biggest in the democratic world. Post-war Sweden saw the development of a universal welfare state offering redistribution of wealth through taxes, transfers and public services. Thus, a good part of the size of the public sector which is usually measured by the percentage of the economy that flows in and out of the public sector as a fraction of the GDP consists of transfers and welfare state programs.

During the early years of globalization, many concerns were raised about the viability of a high-tax, high-spend welfare regime in a globalized economy. As we will discuss in Chapter 3, globalization has entailed a restructuring of the welfare state as taxes and public spending have been reduced, but the defining features of the welfare state have remained. Indeed, some observers argue that the welfare state should be seen less as a weakness in a globalized economy but more as an integrated strategy to cope with globalization as it provides support and compensation in processes of accommodation of global economic pressure and thus facilitates rather than obstructing adaptation (Garrett and Mitchell, 2001; Katzenstein, 1984; but see Olson, 1984). Similarly, Korpi (2003) argues that globalization per se has not challenged the welfare state and that retrenchment in public service is primarily explained by the ascendance of a neoliberal regime in Western Europe.[7]

The result of this economic governance was, at least initially, impressive. Sweden could enjoy a sustained economic growth throughout the post-war period up until 1970 surpassed only by Japan (Krantz, 2008; Lindbeck, 1998). Subsequent decades have provided a more varied picture, and a trajectory of economic development which is more similar to that of the rest of the OECD group of countries. Part of the explanation for this is that the Swedish industry now began to face competition in its core sectors both from Asian countries but also from other European countries. The declining growth has also been attributed to social rigidities, a gradually more militant blue-collar union (the LO) promoting the introduction of so-called wage earners' funds, and instabilities in the oil market (Lindbeck, 1998).[8]

Sweden's post-war political economy has thus been characterized by the interplay between a strong state with a sizeable public sector implementing extensive welfare state programs, a business sector built on a small number of big, internationally oriented companies, and strong organized interests offering protection and compensation for a workforce exposed to international competition (Katzenstein, 1984, 1985).

The more recent political development in Sweden, led by a center-right coalition of parties with the former dominant Social Democratic party playing the role of opposition party, has aimed at getting Sweden out of the high-tax, high-spend economy by cutting taxes and reducing public spending. Although welfare state programs are still generous in international comparison, the government has been able to achieve its core goals in economic policy and can record a better economic performance than most of the EU countries since the global financial crisis hit Sweden in 2008 and later also the euro crisis. Sweden decided to join the EU in the mid-1990s but not the Eurozone; a strategy which in hindsight has protected the Swedish economy from some of the immediate fallout of the euro crisis.

Implemented to some extent by Social Democratic governments but mainly by center-right governments, extensive measures to boost the competitiveness of the Swedish economy have proven successful (see, for instance, *The Economist*, 2013). Thus, in the 2012–2013 Global Competitiveness Index, Sweden is ranked as the fourth most competitive country worldwide, trailing only Switzerland, Singapore, and Finland (Schwab, 2012).[9] Also, in the 2013 KOF Swiss Economic Institute Index of Globalization, Sweden ranks as the 7th most globalized country. By comparison, United States is ranked 35 and Japan ranks at 55th place (KOF, 2013).

## The United States

The American case presents yet another very different picture. As the biggest economy in the world, it displays at any given time elements of almost all stages of the economic development cycle, with some sectors in decline while others are growing. An economy as diverse as that obviously represents in itself a major governance challenge, both in terms of market self-regulation and also the public regulation of sectors of markets (see Campbell et al., 1991). Indeed, the American economy is so diverse both in terms of sectors, maturity and international exposure that it is difficult to make any general statements about "the American economy" beyond standard macroeconomic parameters like inflation, growth, budgetary balance or employment. The post-war period has seen the decline of much of the manufacturing industry, the rapid expansion of the service sector, and the relocation of growth centers from the rustbelt to the coastal areas.

American economic governance is far less interventionist and *dirigiste* than is the case in Sweden and even more so compared to

Japan. Economic governance in the US is, and has historically been, conducted at the level of sectors of the economy and largely left to the market itself with government emphasizing a regulatory role (Campbell et al., 1991). Even at the height of structural problems in the US industry in the 1980s, advocates of a federal industrial policy so successfully designed and implemented by America's key competitors found it extremely difficult to build any support for their ideas. The irony, as several observers have pointed out, was that the US government already implemented programs that could well be defined as industrial policy (see, for instance, Graham, 1992; Nester, 1997:5–13; Weaver, 1985, Ch. 1; Zysman, 1983).

The United States differs in a couple of profound ways from Japan and Sweden in terms of the impact of globalization. American businesses have always had a huge domestic market to rely on and the overwhelming majority of US businesses are not concerned with foreign trade. The US trade dependency is about a quarter of Sweden's, which is a typical small European industrialized democracy (see Figure 1.1). The security and stability which the large domestic market provides was disrupted as free trade and the abolition of trade barriers made its way up the political agenda during the 1980s and 1990s.

Although in principle committed to free trade, the federal government at times has not hesitated to protect the domestic industry from foreign competition in the early post-war period. A case in point is the steel industry which struggled to survive in the face of competition from Europe, Korea and Japan and where tariffs were introduced to help protect the domestic steel producers (Hytrek and Zentgraf, 2008). The list of similar cases would include other previously core sectors of American industry like automobiles, textile, agricultural products and manufactured goods. The creation of NAFTA in 1992 helped speed up the process of economic restructuring by allowing labor-intensive industries to relocate to countries where wages are lower and by allowing for import of foreign products to enter the US markets in free trade. We will return to these issues in Chapter 3, which is devoted to economic governance.

With government refraining from using other instruments than conventional macroeconomic levers such as public spending and interest rates to manipulate the economy, the transformative capacity of the economy in the US is believed to stem from a combination of sound macroeconomic policy and the market-induced change.

* * *

All three countries have experienced some influence of globalization on domestic markets and domestic politics but the accommodation of those global pressures has been rather different, a pattern that continues to date. On closer inspection, there are significant differences between the case countries in terms of their exposure to international markets. Figure 1.1 shows the differences between the three countries we study in terms of their trade dependency. Trade as a fraction of GDP for Japan substantiates the fluctuations in the economy. Japan recorded ratios between 20 and 30 percent in the 1980s with a significant dip beginning in the mid-1980s and continuing through the financially troubled 1990s. As we will discuss in Chapter 3, the appreciation of the yen in the mid-1980s and early 1990s probably contributes to explaining the decreasing trade ratios in Japan. It is not until Japan moved into the third millennium that

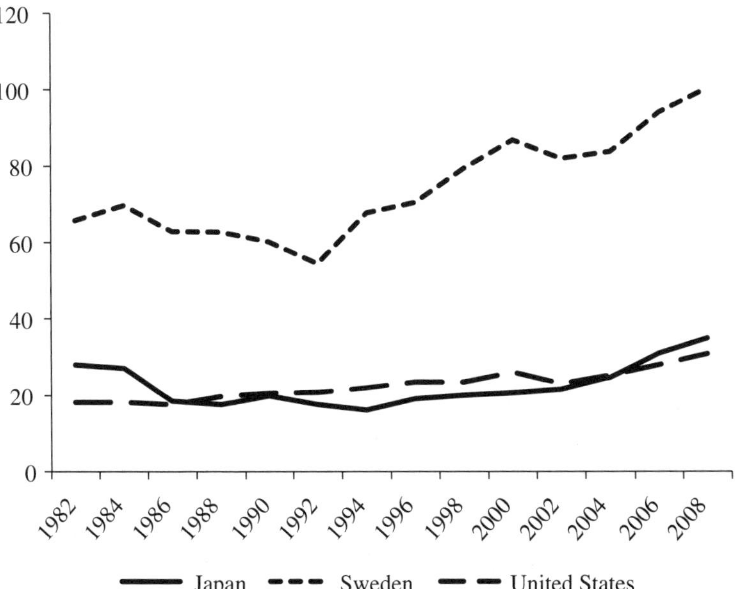


*Source:* OECD StatExtracts.

*Figure 1.1* *Trade-to-GDP ratio. 2012 prices and exchange rates (percentages)*

trade (and the overall economy) began to pick up and reach the levels of the early 1980s. Trade dependency in the United States has been at the same level as Japan's but, unlike Japan, displays a moderate but steady increase from the early 1980s and up to 2008.

Sweden, finally, with its small open economy has seen its trade dependency increase from more than 60 percent in the early 1980s to 100 percent in 2008. Those levels of trade dependency of an advanced industrial democracy highlight the significance of domestic politics of adjustment and compensation as well as political commitments to support the development of competitive concepts and industries.

Thus, for all the three countries, dealing with external contingencies began long before globalization. Trade dependency was significant already in the early 1980s. As advanced industrialized democracies, all three—although Sweden and Japan only more so than the US due to their smaller domestic markets—had for several decades generated large shares of the GDP from trade. Furthermore, all three countries have intensified cooperation and free-trade agreements (ASEAN, NAFTA, EU) in their respective regions. For these countries, then, globalization has meant that their embeddedness in the international economy was taken to a new level, although they already had extensive experience in dealing with that embeddedness (see Kahler and Lake, 2003b:4–7).

* * *

A brief note on the material used in this study would be in order. The analysis draws on a wide variety of material. There is a rich literature on economic governance, inter-governmental relationships, and administrative reform in the three case countries. Most of this literature is however case-based; comparative analyses are surprisingly few. My challenge has been to place these case studies in a comparative perspective in order to uncover and, whenever possible, account for differences among the cases.

In part based on that literature I have conducted series of interviews with experts, officials, and senior civil servants in the three countries. The interviewees are anonymized; this was stated prior to the interviews to offer integrity and allow for candid and non-biased responses. I have consistently chosen to interview civil servants and other officials instead of elected politicians. It is my experience that while politicians may provide good assessments of goals and priorities, civil servants often tend to have better knowledge of actual reform, particularly when observed over time.

The study also draws on a questionnaire study among local governments in the three case countries conducted in 2006. The details of that study are presented in the Appendix. In order to ensure a good response rate I chose to not include a set of items on background data. Instead I ensured that the survey had only a limited number of items. The key purpose of the survey is not to explain variation within or among the case countries but primarily to produce comparable, albeit descriptive, data on local government challenges, their internationalization strategies, and other relevant issues.

In addition to these sources, I have relied on government documents, material provided by national associations of local and regional government and numerous informal discussions with country experts on how to interpret reform in different sectors.

## CONCLUDING COMMENTS

The globalization debate continues to be heated. Skeptics portray the deregulation of the international economy as a triumph of the economy over political institutions while the advocates of reform insist that free trade and mobility of resources will bring prosperity to all.

Social scientists are still grappling with how to assess the multidimensional and contradictory phenomenon of globalization. A final and conclusive assessment of the empirical extent and normative desirability of globalization is of course impossible. The position of the present study is that the perhaps most rewarding approach is to zero in on specific issues in specific sectors in a few case countries in order to uncover the interactions between the global (in whatever shape it may manifest itself) and the domestic. By studying these micro-foundations of globalization we can understand the process through which international or global norms are inserted into domestic politics. Again, this strategy will not yield a comprehensive account of globalization but it will generate some insights into the complexities of domestic decision-making in a globalizing world.

The three countries selected for the study are all affluent democracies; some might say that this is a comparison of three of the winners of globalization. However, the political and bureaucratic leaders of the three countries would probably agree that they have experienced both the best of times and worst of the times in a globalizing world. Yet, their story is vastly different from those told by their colleagues in developing countries. These are caveats which should be borne in mind as we study the impact of globalization on the three countries.

## NOTES

1. Certainly, there are also skeptics who maintain that globalization is exaggerated and provide empirical evidence. that economies are still predominantly national, governed and regulated by domestic political institutions (see, for instance, Garrett, 1995; Hirst and Thompson, 1999; Keohane and Milner, 1996; Mosley, 2003; Swank, 2002).
2. Research on convergence in the 1990s produced very different results. Thus for instance, about half of the contributors to Berger and Dore's volume *National Diversity and Global Capitalism* (Berger and Dore, 1996) found strong evidence of convergence whereas the others did not.
3. Welfare-state policies is one of very few sectors that would have been relevant in this governance perspective, partly because of the extensive debate on the future of the welfare state in a globalized world and partly because it includes all levels of government and also (increasingly) relates to the market as a service provider and a complement to public social insurance. However, these issues have been extensively researched. The results are ambiguous but suggest overall that welfare states have proven resilient to globalization. Cutbacks in welfare services and programs during the 1980s and 1990s should be attributed more to the ascendance of neo-liberal governments in several Western European countries and less to globalization per se (see Genschel, 2004; Glatzer and Rueschemeyer, 2005; Korpi, 2003; Steinmo, 2012).
4. As we will see in Chapter 5, Americans do not see their administrative reform as typical of NPM but rather a more home-grown model of "Reinvention" based in the National Performance Review program.
5. Interestingly, the selection of cases is identical to that used by Sven Steinmo in his book on how these three countries have adapted to globalization. However, Steinmo does not look specifically at the three sectors chosen in the present study. Also, Steinmo's study draws on evolutionary theory which is not the case for our analysis.
6. There were however aspects of the deregulated global economy which the Swedish government had not anticipated. In 1992, the country faced a major financial crisis as the currency market speculated aggressively against the Swedish Krona. It seems clear that the government had failed to anticipate that a pegged currency combined with a growing budget deficit could trigger such speculation. See Chapter 3 and Pierre, 1999.
7. It could be argued that globalization played an important role in shaping domestic policy choice by calling for policies that conform to the neo-liberal regime, in which case globalization is causally related to welfare-state retrenchment. Although clearly relevant, that issue falls outside the immediate scope of the present project.
8. The Swedish post-war trajectory of economic development has been the topic of a heated argument among economists and social scientists, a debate that has

academic as well as political dimensions. See Krantz, 2008 and the literature cited therein.

9. Indeed, in a composite index of global competitiveness, ease of doing business, global innovation, corruption perception, and human development, *The Economist* (2013) ranked Sweden, Denmark, Finland, and Norway as the top-four countries worldwide.

# 2. Globalization and domestic governance

> If we want things to stay as they are, things will have to change.
> Guiseppe Tomasi di Lampedusa (1958), *The Leopard*

> Thomas Jefferson believed that to perceive the very foundation of our nation we would need to change from time to time. Well, my fellow Americans, this is our time. Let us embrace it.
> Bill Clinton, first inaugural address, 1993

Globalization brought with it new types of pressure on the state and the domestic economy. Economic liberalization exposed domestic companies to global competition while domestic institutions were urged by international political and institutional actors to implement policies of trade liberalization and market deregulation. These two drivers of policy change merged into an overarching reassessment of the capabilities and roles of the state in governance, of macroeconomic policy, and of state–market relations. The change in discourse of macroeconomic policy in the industrialized world from that of Keynesianism, Bretton Woods, and the "strong societies" of the 1950s and 1960s to the monetarism, IMF, and the "enabling state" model of the 1990s and 2000s could not have been more profound.

This chapter will investigate the relationship between globalization and domestic governance by analysing the political and economic pressures on domestic governance that globalization entails and the domestic processes through which those processes are accommodated. In the previous chapter we briefly touched on the different linkages between global economic forces and domestic politics. The chapter goes further into that discussion before the next three chapters study the three themes and case countries which are central to the empirical analysis.

The chapter first describes different types of globalization pressures on the state. This section focuses on two such pressures. One is the influence of international capital that followed after the deregulation of domestic financial markets. The other type of international pressure is related to international financial institutions such as the International Monetary Fund (IMF), the World Bank, the Inter-American Development Bank (IDB), the OECD, and the World Trade Organization (WTO). These institutions exercise considerable influence over individual states, not least in the context of providing aid and assistance during financial crises.

The chapter then turns to a discussion on different domestic strategies to cope with these international pressures. We focus specifically on four such strategies: regional cooperation; protecting domestic markets and penetrating markets overseas; relaxing domestic institutional hierarchies; and policy change.

## GLOBALIZING PRESSURES ON THE STATE

The 1980s and 1990s presented nation states with new types of external contingencies to which they had to relate; political and economic pressures directly or indirectly set in motion by the increasing mobility of capital, ideas, people, and services. During these decades, the advanced Western democracies embarked on an extensive project of deregulating their economies, thus integrating their financial markets with those of other countries. Much of this reform was implemented with direct reference to globalization (Weiss, 1998). The emerging global economy opened up new markets and provided increased cross-border mobility. At the same time it delocalized labor-intensive manufacturing to low-cost labor countries, thus redefining the competitive edge of many countries. Nation states therefore struggled to devise a strategy that would help them maximize the benefits of globalization while minimizing the costs. The more specific details of that strategy varied significantly across national contexts, as we will see.

This was also a time when the political leadership paid close attention to the financial market's reactions to policy proposals or even to senior political appointments. "The market" rather suddenly emerged as an anonymous but influential point of reference in political debate and decision making. In Sweden during the financially tumultuous 1990s, the political leadership took great caution not to launch policies that would work against what were believed to be the interests of "the market". As the then Prime Minister Göran Persson told the present author in an interview in 1997 (Pierre, 1999:24): "You have to ask yourself what is going on when you immediately after giving a press conference rush back to your office and turn on page 234 on Teletext to see how the market reacts . . . However, as the national debt is decreasing our degrees of freedom have increased."

It was not clear whether "the market" was global or domestic but it had over a very brief period of time become a force clearly to be reckoned with, and to which policy had to relate; policies or appointments that did not please the market drove interest rates up and exchanges rates down. For the political leaderships of countries like Japan or Sweden with their long tradition of deliberating policy with key societal partners (Pempel and Tsunekawa, 1979; Öberg, 1994), the notion of having a new and extremely influential actor yet anonymous and thus not present at the bargaining table was probably daunting. Fortunately, this state of affairs would not be a permanent feature. The Swedish government devoted the 1990s to restoring budgetary balance, and the most immediate and powerful manifestations of market influence on policy declined.

The increasing inward mobility of labor was another source of uncertainty. In the advanced European welfare states politicians and bureaucrats feared that the free trade of goods, capital, labor and services in the EU would lead to "welfare tourism", where foreigners would collect welfare state benefits without making contributions to the tax base; a concern that would soon prove to have been greatly exaggerated. Unions in these countries also worried that low-cost labor from new EU member states would enter the labor market on a large scale, disrupting wage development and undermining union strength. Again, while the expansion of the EU did open up the previously fairly closed labor markets in Western Europe, the initial fears of wage dumping would prove exaggerated.

Thus, across Western Europe there was concern that the continuing EU integration coupled with financial deregulation would have a combined impact on the political economy that would significantly challenge the welfare state. The extensive research on the impact of globalization on the welfare state, however, seems to disprove those concerns. Reviewing this body of research, Genschel (2004:632) concludes that:

> [G]lobalization as a phenomenological and causal whole is being deconstructed. The hope of finding in it a meta-variable that accounts in simple, law-like fashion for all the problems and changes of advanced welfare states over the past thirty years has been abandoned . . . This is not to say that globalization is irrelevant. It just means that political reactions to globalization are not entirely preprogrammed by globalization itself but also depend on domestic structures.

Genshel's observation is valid not only for the advanced welfare states. It echoes Weiss' (1998) previously discussed argument that the impact of globalization is to a large extent a function of domestic institutions and strategies.

Thus, Genschel and Weiss both highlight the interactive dimension of globalization where pressures and domestic resilience strategies decide the outcome of international pressures on the state. Let us now turn to an analysis of such pressures. The two perhaps most frequently discussed challenges to the state triggered by globalization are those that are related to the deregulation of financial markets and, secondly, the role of transnational organizations in promoting domestic reform to promote free trade and global access to domestic markets. We will discuss these two issues in turn.

**Deregulation of Financial Markets**

Financial globalization, according to Frenkel (2003:40), has two mutually reinforcing dimensions; the increasing flow of financial transactions across borders, and "the sequence of institutional and legal reforms implemented to liberalize and deregulate international capital movements and national financial systems". Financial institutions and markets in the US and UK were among the first to see their regulatory frameworks being relaxed. With those powerful economies leading the way, most of the advanced industrialized democracies believed they had little choice but to follow suit in order to keep a level playing field in the competition for international investment.

As we will see in more detail in the next chapter, Japan, Sweden, and the US present different cases of the causes and consequences of this reform. For now, suffice it to say that the US, as one of the avant-garde countries in the deregulation process, embarked and pursued its deregulation under very limited overseas pressure. Japan had begun privatization of state-owned companies and limited deregulation in the 1980s but came under substantive pressure from international organizations such as the IMF and the World Bank to deregulate its financial sector in the 1990s as a component of its strategy to address its financial crises during that decade (Amyx, 2004; see Chapter 3). Sweden, finally, decided—somewhat out of character—to deregulate its financial markets with very little analysis of what that would mean in terms of domestic control and vulnerability to global economic pressure. The result was a major financial crisis in 1992, triggered by aggressive speculation against the Krona (Dennis, 1998; Hinnfors and Pierre, 1998; Lundgren, 1998; Telasuo, 2000).

These types of economic pressures had not been felt before by the governments of Japan and Sweden. Their predicament was soon to be shared by the governments of Korea (1997–1998), Malaysia (1997), Finland (1991), and Argentina (2001), just to give a few examples (Frenkel, 2003; Kim and Kim, 2003; Yusoff et al., 2000).[1] Thus this was a type of financial crisis that was primarily and directly triggered by financial globalization. Other models of financial crises include the 2008 crisis in Iceland driven by high-risk financial management strategies by commercial banks and the 2012 crisis in Spain brought about by a bubble economy. These crises were caused by behavior enabled by deregulation which in turn is related to globalization, and the process through which they evolved was different from international speculation against a country's currency or financial balance (see Krugman, 1994b).

Martin Wolf (2008) points out that "the epoch of globalisation has been an epoch of financial crises" (but see Reinhart and Rogoff, 2008). Given the close global interdependencies among banks and financial institutions, a crisis in one country's financial sector will almost automatically have international repercussions; the only question is how soon and how powerful will those repercussions be. The financial crisis which originated in the American real estate and financial markets in 2008, spread across the world almost instantly as several US financial institutions either collapsed or had to be bailed out by the federal government. The crisis showed once again how closely intertwined national financial markets and institutions are.

In terms of domestic policy and governance choice, the most significant novelty of this type of globalization was that it created a new and powerful source and driver of policy which was exogenous to the domestic political system. Governments were exposed to several different types of policy pressures at once. Financial deregulation meant that economies which suffered from deficits, “bubbles” in their real estate market or major structural problems could become targets of overseas speculation. Facing that risk—its awesome powers already demonstrated in several cases—government should maintain a strict fiscal and budgetary discipline and macroeconomic policy.

Furthermore, there was also the broader, more general reference to globalization in political discourse according to which domestic policy would have to prioritize cutbacks in public budgets and taxes and deregulate domestic markets (Hay and Rosamond, 2002; Weiss, 1998). These policy measures were believed to be integral to protect the domestic economy from international speculation against the currency and to maintain competitiveness for global investment capital. Thus, in the globalization discourse this neo-liberal policy “turn” was presented less as a choice but more as a necessary adaptation to the new political and economic circumstances (Steinmo, 2012).

These manifestations of the pressures that deregulated international financial markets could put on national governments helped in many cases instill a tighter fiscal and budgetary control. The early 1990s saw finance ministries in several Western democracies take a higher political profile and ascend to a position from where they effectively could control other departments; a position they have since then not surrendered (see, e.g. Jensen, 2003). However, trade liberalization also offered new industrial ventures and opened up new markets for raw materials and consumer goods.

## Transnational Institutions

Pressures from transnational institutions on domestic political choice could certainly be viewed as external impositions on the state but the matter is more complex than it might appear to be at first. Transnational organizations like the World Bank, the International Monetary Fund (IMF), the World Trade Organization (WTO), the OECD, and the Inter-American Development Bank (IDB) are essentially collective institutions created to solve common problems and to muster financial and regulatory capabilities required to assist individual countries either in times of crisis or to aid their more long-term economic development (see Stiglitz, 2003).

The WTO has a mission not only to settle trade disputes and promote free trade but also to promote domestic deregulation (Hoekman and Kostecki, 1995) with, as the organization's mission statement puts it, "justifiable exceptions or with adequate flexibilities".[2] The degree to which the WTO can interfere with domestic regulatory arrangements is a somewhat delicate issue. Member states are complied to adhere with the WTO's policy of deregulation but even so it is not always clear to what extent specific regulations are in violation with such policy.

During the heyday of promoting "good governance" in the 1980s and early 1990s (Leftwich, 1994; Pierre and Peters, 2000), the IMF and the World Bank would occasionally condition support and aid on domestic reform aiming at opening up markets to overseas companies. This "conditionality" was also used when putting together rescue packages to countries in financial crisis. Everyone did not applaud this strategy. Joseph Stiglitz, one of the critics of conditionality, notes that "[T]hose who valued democratic processes saw how 'conditionality'—the conditions that international lenders imposed in return for their assistance—undermined national sovereignty" (Stiglitz, 2003:9). Stiglitz even goes so far as to argue that conditionality often proved to be counterproductive.

There is also a matter of ethics involved in conditioning aid to countries in crisis on specific domestic reforms. As Martin Feldstein (1998:27) suggests, apropos the IMF's rescue support to Korea in 1997, "the fundamental issue is the appropriate role for an international agency and its technical staff in dealing with sovereign countries that come to it for assistance". Feldstein argued that conditioning aid and help on domestic policy change was taking advantage of the recipient country's distress and did not resonate with the basic ethics of helping someone in jeopardy. Feldstein's point is that the aid and support which the IMF offers to countries in crisis is not value-neutral but has distinct neo-liberal objectives which the recipient country has little choice but to accept in order to receive financial assistance.

Similar models of conditionality have also manifested themselves, through the "Washington Consensus", in recommendations from the World Bank and the IMF to recipient countries in Latin America and Asia to deregulate the domestic economy, open up domestic markets, and conduct policy more in accordance with Western, predominantly American, liberal norms and ideals (see Chapter 1; also, see Philippi, 2003; Serra and Stiglitz, 2008; Stiglitz, 2003). Observing the IMF's aid to Japan in the 1990s, Glenn Hook argues: "While not as such a direct attack on the Japanese model, the IMF policies essentially served to spread the liberal project pursued by the US and undermine the Japanese model by calling for changes meant to erode the basic premise of the model" (Hook, 2001:46).

Thus, understanding the diffusion and adoption of international norms and ideas is not merely a matter of uncovering those domestic processes; it is also a matter of understanding the wider logic of how and why and by whom such ideas are set in international motion. Subsequent chapters will show that most of the models, concepts, and ideas that were brought into domestic governance reform in Japan and Sweden emanated from the United States, either bilaterally or through international organizations such as the IMF, the OECD or the World Bank.

The external pressure for change could also be subtle and indirect, as is the case in the diffusion of international standards and norms (Brunsson and Jacobsson, 2000). It could also be extremely influential and non-negotiable, as was the case with the firm prescriptions from transnational organizations like the EU and the IMF on the Greek government to implement extensive austerity programs during the financial crisis in 2011 and 2012.

Let us now turn our attention to the other side of the global-domestic exchanges and discuss different strategies of containment and adaptation to international political and economic pressures.

## THE POLITICS AND STRATEGIES OF ADAPTATION

If globalization, either in and of itself or as a catalyst of other transformative drivers, confronted the state with a partially new set of powerful challenges, it also presented a major impetus for states to rethink policy and to design and implement economic and other policies that were appropriate for the new global political landscape. As a result, the past few decades have witnessed a process of adaptation and learning on the side of the political and administrative leaderships around the world.

The idea that states respond to globalization by adapting their domestic governance arrangements has been a significant feature in international political economy, administrative reform, and comparative politics. It has been less common to link that argument to the discussion about state strength and the purported decline of the state in the face of globalization. Guy Peters argues that many scholars have tended to underestimate the adaptive capacity of the state; "much of the denigration of the governing capacity of the traditional nation state is a function of adopting a static view of governments and their abilities to make policies that meet posited goals" (Peters, 2000:43). However, although there is good reason to assume that states are indeed capable of adapting a new globalizing environment, adaptation is a process fraught with uncertainties and unknown variables and is therefore often insufficient or properly designed or even appropriate, given the nature of the external pressure (see Olsen, 2010:198); "adaptation is myopic, meandering, and 'inefficient'; it does not generate a uniquely optimal arrangement".

In that context of uncertainty, then, the most immediate issue confronting governments around the world in the 1980s was to identify which political and economic factors define the scope of domestic policy and governance choice in a globalizing world, and what political, institutional and economic conditions increase exposure to international markets and speculation based on parameters in the economy (real estate price development, interest rates, inflation, currency exchange rates, national debt, and so on). Based on that analysis, governments could form a strategy which would control the risk of overseas penetration of markets at the same time as it set the long-term objectives for the state in a globalizing economy, for example promoting inward investment; helping domestic businesses to explore international markets; recruiting skilled labor and experts in key emerging industries; preventing corporate relocation out of the country, and so on.

However, globalization did not come into existence overnight and neither did the political response to globalization. States could not reinvent their economy but, in the short term, had to play the hand they were given. Thus, different national economies generated different strategies to manage globalization. Fritz Scharpf (1998:3) argues that:

> increasing competition on product and service markets will presumably lead to different national responses. Countries with unfavorable starting conditions—like, for instance, the UK at the end of the seventies—may

> have to opt for cost reductions and deregulation. Other countries, however, may have a choice between the British low-cost strategy and strategies that would increase their comparative advantages in terms of productivity, quality and innovation.

Coming back to a point made earlier, this pattern suggests that convergence is not a useful measure of global influences on domestic policy choice, as national economies began their adjustment to the globalized economy from vastly different structural preconditions and levels of economic development. Trade liberalization exposed businesses, sometimes whole industries, to international competition and thus hastened the process of structural change. This pattern was most noticeable in former Central and Eastern Europe but could be seen across the industrialized world. Some companies were shut down as a result of the new global economy; other, more viable businesses, would consider relocating to countries with lower levels of corporate taxation. Both processes contributed to a restructuring of the domestic economy in the industrialized democracies.

The prospect of corporate relocation is but one of many issues where the economic dimension of globalization connects with its political dimension. Indeed, it is the aggregate political and economic influence that globalization places on the state that is at the heart of the globalization debate. To some observers, the result is a scenario characterized by economy over politics, structure over agency, and discourse over choice. The more extreme version of the globalization argument holds that in order not to lose competitiveness states have to cater to the interests of global financial capital by reducing public expenditure, cutting taxes and deregulating domestic markets. This analysis is sometimes made without explicit political reference but in a more matter-of-fact fashion (Steinmo, 2012), almost as a new natural law of politics.

Critics of this deterministic view suggest that the causality between domestic regulatory dismantling and international competitiveness has yet to be demonstrated; that the ideological foundation of the globalization discourse must be recognized as a normative position rather than an objective, empirical position; and that the impact of globalization on any given state is the result of domestic political and institutional factors as much as of the nature of global pressures (see, for instance, Amoore et al., 1997; Boyer and Drache, 1996; Camilleri and Falk, 1992; Hirst and Thompson, 1999; Weiss, 1998).

In order to understand the economic and political influence on domestic policy choice, two important issues should be borne in mind. First, despite the comprehensive, all-embracing connotation of globalization, much of what we commonly see as manifestations of globalization does not affect all countries, and does not affect countries in similar ways or with similar outcomes, owing to differences in the structure of the economy and the level of development (see Section II in Kahler and Lake, 2003a; Weiss, 1998). For instance, the deregulation of domestic raw material markets presents a potential problem to countries whose economy is predominantly based in the exploitation of natural resources. The same deregulation offers opportunities for countries with companies adding value to natural resources. In the same way, deregulating domestic financial markets affects countries quite differently owing to what composes the domestic economy and its exposure to international markets. Some countries have the institutional and political leverage to resist global pressures, others are transmitters of global pressures and yet other countries are left with little choice than to respond to globalization more or less regardless of the domestic ramifications.

Secondly, the influence of the globalization discourse on domestic policy choice depends on the degree to which the political norms and values of globalization resonate with the ideological orientation of the domestic regime. Global pressures for opening up markets for international investment or deregulating financial markets and labor markets obviously play to those domestic political parties that share the neo-liberal political orientation. Market-supporting and neo-liberal regimes will be less obstructive towards international norms of trade liberalization and deregulation compared to regimes of a more leftist political leaning. Countries governed by regimes based in universal welfare provision and redistribution of wealth tend to enforce a stricter regulatory framework on markets and are therefore more tentative towards overseas recommendations to "liberate" domestic markets and reduce public spending. The ideological orientation of the regime matters in several ways. Social democratic regimes prioritize the compensation of labor for international market exposure to a higher degree than other regimes (Garrett, 1995; Katzenstein, 1984; Ruggie, 1998).

With regard to international financial institutions, their influence on individual states seems to be highly contextualized; a national economy with strong institutions and in good balance does not lend itself to the same overseas pressure as a poorly managed economy. The past decade has shown that countries that asked for assistance from the IMF during the 1990s have gone to great lengths to avoid a repetition of that calamity, by exercising tight fiscal and budgetary discipline.

The embeddedness of the state in its international environment, including international aid organizations, offers opportunities as well as contingencies. While international financial institutions tend to have reform agendas attached to their aid, they do offer protection against aggressive market speculation and mitigate other forms of global pressures from non-accountable actors. From the point of view of the state, then, a strategic objective in relation to these institutions could be to minimize the risk of being dependent on their support while maximizing the opportunities they offer.

## Towards Collective Action: Regional Cooperation

The first strategy of adaptation we will discuss is regional cooperation, that is, neighboring countries creating free-trade areas or other forms of joint, collective strategies of action. Globalization presents national economies with a highly competitive environment. The industrialized democracies have a long history of dealing with the contingencies that international markets pose to the state. The emergence of deregulated financial markets and dismantled trade barriers exacerbated those contingencies. Regional international cooperation follows a similar pattern; there are cases of such cooperation that date far back in time (the Hanseatic League in Northern Europe dating back to the thirteenth century arguably being one of the first international free-trade communities) but globalization has served as a powerful incentive towards the formation or expansion of regional free trade zones or other patterns of regional cooperation.

Regional cooperation is an umbrella term for a variety of such initiatives with different objectives and different degrees of institutionalization. The most advanced example of regional integration is the European Union. For the EU member states, creating a union of sovereign states caters to a number of political and economic objectives, one of which is collective security. Regional trade alliances, like Mercosur, NAFTA, APEC[3] and ASEAN[4] create favorable trading conditions in a controlled environment and may give the region a stronger voice vis-à-vis international financial institutions.

The emergence of an East Asian region, Paul Evans (2005) argues, is more a manifestation of regionalization—an institutionalized regional governance to facilitate stronger economic development for the countries in the region—than of regionalism, that is, a shared regional identity. Even so, ASEAN is planning an economic community by 2015, further strengthening trade in the region and regional economic development and competitiveness (Basu Das, 2012).

Regional cooperation appears to be a cumulative process; regionalization in one part of the world seems to drive similar processes in other areas as a strategy of adaptation to the globalized, and at the same time regionalized, economy (Katzenstein, 2005). For instance, the growing regional integration in Europe was used by President Clinton in the negotiations towards NAFTA to drive home the need for the countries on the North American continent to create similar conditions for cross-border trade (Spulber, 1995:224–5). Few countries want to go it alone in a globalized economy, particularly when other countries deepen their collaboration. That having been said, regional cooperation is not only a matter of safety by numbers. Indeed, most regional free-trade zones are little more than a regulatory framework for trade within the region. It is also important to note that while transnational institutions offer some protection against global economic pressures, member states must commit themselves to them and the regime that they represent in order for regional cooperation to be effective (Schmidt, 1999).

These processes towards regional cooperation are causal responses to globalization (Katzenstein, 2005; Pempel, 2005; Schaede and Grimes, 2003b). The close linkage between globalization and regionalization was emphasized by a METI official in an interview in 2005:

> There is now a free trade area in the Asian region. There have been several new cases of regional cooperation in the Southeast Asian region during the past several years. Such regional cooperation is a very direct response to globalization . . . In the next ten years we will need to think more about globalization. A few years ago we worried about delocalization to China. Today we work *with* the Chinese.[5]

The logic of regional cooperation as a response to globalization is that free trade within a controlled space allows countries to boost economic development without engaging in global competition. It is a response which thus enables countries to extract the benefits of globalization without exposing themselves to the contingencies of global economic pressures. The optimal outcome is when all parties benefit from penetrating each other's' domestic markets.

**Protecting the Local, Shaping the Global: "Permeable Insulation"**

In a broader, strategic perspective, the state has two overarching objectives as it adapts to the global economy and global politics. The first objective is to prevent a global flow of goods into the domestic market which would significantly increase competition, possibly with severe ramifications on domestic producers. Secondly, given the pressure from transnational donors and financial institutions, the state—as any institution confronted with a volatile environment—has strong incentives to "enact its environment" (March and Olsen, 1989) and engage these actors in order to influence its external environment and to be able to predict its developments. The capacity to implement such a strategy is contingent on a range of factors such as the capability of the state to influence international trade regulation and its capacity to facilitate and accommodate domestic change and adaptation.

Most of the advanced industrialized democracies have attempted to implement this strategy albeit with varying degrees of success. Protecting domestic markets from overseas competition during a global free-trade regime and engaging international institutions as a means of gaining control over the state's international environment requires clout and leverage in international arenas and domestic political and bureaucratic skill. Schaede and Grimes and their associates (2003b) argue that Japan's response to globalization is a successful example of what they call "permeable insulation".

Schaede and Grimes deserve to be quoted at some length:

> 'Permeable insulation' means that Japan's response to the global and domestic challenges of the 1990s is neither one of retreat and denial, nor one of full acceptance of global standards and practices. Instead, the basic thrust is one of pragmatic utilization of new rules and circumstances to continue industry policies of promotion and protection in a new, post-developmental, paradigm. Moreover, the approach sees Japan, for the first time in memory, as an active player in actually shaping the international environment through political and legal means, rather than simply reacting to real or perceived shocks. This new approach of shifting its insulation strategies to global or regional frameworks is one of the most important facets of Japan's response to the global and political pressures of the twenty-first century. (Schaede and Grimes, 2003b:8)[6]

Thus, Japan's strategy in facing up to the continuing globalization became more proactive as globalization progressed. As financial markets were deregulated and trade barriers gradually removed (a topic of increasingly heated bilateral or multilateral arguments), Japan opened up those domestic markets where overseas impact would be manageable. At the same time, Japan became more active in pursuing its political and strategic goals internationally. The financial crisis in the 1990s and the ensuing need for overseas assistance increased Japan's vulnerability to pressures from international institutions. However, as we will see in the next chapter, Japan has also learned how to use those institutions and their aid to other countries for its own purpose. Schaede and Grimes' analysis thus echoes Linda Weiss's (1998) finding that the strength and impact of globalization depends on domestic institutional arrangements and that the governing capacity of the state is derived not only from its institutions but also from its ability to manage international interdependencies (Weiss, 1998).

This strategy of protecting domestic markets while penetrating markets in other countries was not new. Japan excelled in this trade policy during the prosperous 1960s and 1970s. The United States, a strong advocate of free trade and the removal of tariffs and other barriers to trade, has been successful in protecting its domestic markets in agricultural products from overseas competition, for example from developing countries (Stiglitz, 2003). Sweden, given its high trade dependency and small size, has had difficulties in imposing trade barriers but has instead chosen to compensate domestic constituencies exposed to international competition and to increase flexibility in the labor market.

Instead, the novelty of this approach, at least for Japan, lies in the combination of protecting the domestic economy while actively seeking to influence key actors in its environment. The United States, partly as a result of the weight it can throw in bilateral or multilateral trade negotiations and partly as a result of Washington Consensus policies, has been able to shape its external environment to a considerable degree. Sweden, by contrast, is a small player in global negotiations and has had little choice but to do what it perhaps does best; to develop competitiveness in key sectors of industry and research and to adapt to fluctuations in international markets.

**Rescaling and Institutional Change**

The above types of responses to globalization refer to adaptation in the form of changing political objectives such as a stricter fiscal and budgetary policy or creating regional frameworks for states to act collectively. In addition to these forms of adaptation, globalization induces change or adaptation in domestic institutional systems (Amoore et al., 1997; Cerny, 1990; Jayasuria, 2002). The present analysis will not be able to probe very deeply into this discourse. Instead, we will concentrate on how globalization impacts the relation among domestic institutions, particularly the relationship between central, regional, and local government.

Neil Brenner (1999, 2004) suggests that globalization tends to "rescale" political authority within the state so that the hierarchical order is replaced by a functional division of authority and roles between the state, regions, and cities. This means that subnational government becomes less constrained by the domestic institutional hierarchy and can pursue their interests in international arenas. The era of globalization has indeed been one of institutional restructuring such as subnational internationalization; insulation of national banks; expansion of regulatory agencies; increasing international embeddedness in institutional hierarchies such as the EU; and the emergence of transnational or regional governance arrangements.

Two issues arise, however, as we observe these developments against the backdrop of globalization. One issue is related to assigning causality; to what extent were these institutional changes linked to globalization and to what degree were they driven by other forces, for example a neo-liberal "turn", decentralization reform, or fiscal cutbacks to subnational government? While it appears clear that central bank reform and the increasing power of finance ministries in many countries are explained by a need to insulate fiscal policy from parochial pressures and tighten control over public expenditure, the emergence of subnational government on international arenas and the relaxation of domestic institutional hierarchies more broadly are less easy to relate causally to globalization (see Chapter 4).

The other issue has to do with agency; as Goldfinch and t'Hart (2003:236) remind us, "[R]eforms, like decisions, do not just 'happen'". They challenge entrenched interests and norms and require significant drivers to bring about change. Again, the political reform that globalization entailed had clear objectives and was driven by (for the most part) neo-liberal regimes in the advanced Western democracies. The "rescaling" argument, on the other hand, is phrased in a more passive language, identifying changes but not the agents driving them. Subnational internationalization is clearly tied to globalization, directly by incentivizing cities and regions to seek strategic alliances overseas and indirectly through the neo-liberal policy of encouraging competition among cities and regions (see Chapter 5). Agency in the rescaling model is thus presumably partly tied to national government and partly to subnational institutions, seizing the opportunity to pursue their objectives internationally at a time when the financial support from the state is gradually reduced.

## Policy Change

A fourth type of adaptive behavior of states is adapting policy to changing external preconditions. Throughout this chapter we have emphasized the complexities involved with this type of adaption, both in terms of the uncertainties of what constitutes "good policy" in a globalizing world and also in terms of the adaptive capacity of the state. Subsequent chapters will discuss relevant cases of policy change in three countries under study. However, since the focus of the present academic enterprise is on the impact of globalization on domestic governance arrangements and not on domestic policy, we will not go into any detail on that issue.

That said, we note that globalization incentivizes the state to reassess not only policy and governance arrangements but also its arsenal of policy instruments. Cut-back policies have meant that countries that previously relied on subsidies to subnational government as a steering instrument, for example Japan, now has turned to other, "softer" instruments in the central–local institutional relationship. Furthermore, as Marc Eisner points out, "globalization poses vexing problems for regulation" because "national institutions cannot regulate international markets nor can genuinely international institutions fill the vacuum unless nations are prepared to relinquish some of their sovereignty" (Eisner, 2000:203, 222). Regulation, which interestingly is often considered to be one of the key instruments available to the state in a globalized context, remains an important policy instrument but its efficiency in steering society declines with the increasing international embeddedness of the state.

Furthermore, transnational influences on domestic institutions can sometimes serve as drivers of domestic policy change which has been prevented by organized interests. For instance, the Maastricht Treaty and the Stability and Growth Pact in the EU have probably assisted national governments both in putting certain types of economic reform on the political agenda and also to fend off domestic special interests seeking to obstruct such reform. Similarly, a METI[7] official in Japan describes the situation thus, apropos the role of the WTO in influencing domestic agricultural reform and the differences between bilateral and multilateral trade negotiations: "Contingency on international institutions can also be a good thing, not just a bad thing. We can use those institutions to persuade domestic constituencies. US pressures alone are not enough to persuade Japanese farmers."[8] Thus, external pressures for policy change may provide windows of opportunity for such change and can provide the momentum to enforce a new course of policy which otherwise would not have been possible.

* * *

The two main types of global pressures on domestic governance discussed above—the powers of international financial actors unleashed by the deregulation of domestic financial markets and the influence exercised by international financial institutions—will be investigated empirically in Chapters 3–5. These chapters will also assess how the three case countries employ the different strategies of adaptation—regional cooperation, "permeable insulation", institutional change in the shape of rescaling of political authority, and policy change—to mitigate the impact of globalization. Again, since the core theme of the book is on domestic governance reform, not policy, we will not assess policy change as a discrete category of domestic adaptation. The other types of adaptation will play a bigger role. Regional cooperation and "permeable insulation" will be further analysed in Chapter 3 on economic governance, and rescaling is central to the analysis on changing inter-governmental relationships in Chapter 4. Chapter 5, on administrative reform, continues the analysis of institutional change in the context of public administration and public management.

Observing three sectors of domestic governance in three different national contexts, we investigate the extent to which reform has been driven by exogenous factors which can be related to global pressures, or if the trajectory of domestic reform is path-dependent, that is, reflective of long-term national political and administrative practices. We furthermore study in as much detail as the material allows us what have been the main drivers of reform and through which processes overseas ideas and norms have been integrated with domestic governance reform.

## OUTLINING A FRAMEWORK FOR ANALYSIS: PATH-DEPENDENT REFORM OR ADAPTING TO GLOBAL PRESSURES?

Table 2.1 presents the basic features of the three countries covered in the analysis.

The three countries differ significantly in terms of their institutional arrangements and also the timeline of their reforms. The three cases lend themselves to comparing two against the third. Japan and the US are large countries, economic superpowers, and "price makers" (Katzenstein, 1985) while Sweden is a "price taker"; a much smaller economy where trade dependency is more marked than in the other two systems. Furthermore, following Hall and Soskice we could say that Japan and Sweden are both coordinated market economies whereas the United States is a typical liberal market economy (Hall and Soskice, 2001). On the other hand, Japan and Sweden have a number of similarities in terms of their economic affluence, their parliamentary system of government and their egalitarian culture (Krauss and Pierre, 1990).

With three sectors in three national contexts we thus conduct and compare nine case studies. This organizational structure allows us to conduct comparison either among different sectors of domestic governance within the same country or comparing the same sector across the three different countries. It is the latter strategy which is pursued in this book hence the thematic organization of the book rather than a country-by-country structure. Thus we use a simple analytical framework focusing on three policy sectors (economic governance, administrative reform, and inter-governmental relationships) in three countries (Japan, Sweden, and the United States).

Each of the case studies asks whether the reform that characterizes the sector is path-dependent with the long-term trajectory of change (in which case we argue that globalization has not

*Table 2.1 Japan, Sweden and USA: basic characteristics*

| | Japan | Sweden | United States |
|---|---|---|---|
| Institutional system | Unitary state with weak local government | Unitary state with strong local government | Federal state with fragmented local government |
| Economic governance | Market economy with significant political intervention and regulation | "Mixed economy" with moderate intervention and big public sector | Market economy with some regulation |
| Economic deregulation | 1990s, partial reform | Late 1980s, primarily financial markets | Early 1980s, extensive deregulation |
| Administrative system | Central ministries, some agencies | Department and autonomous agencies | Department and executive agencies |

significantly altered domestic governance) or if reforms during the past couple of decades have meant a profound break with that trajectory (in which case we suggest that globalization has had a significant impact on domestic reform). We will also, in as much detail as possible, investigate the causal drivers of such policy change to see if those drivers were mainly domestic or international. Given the scope of each case analysis, however, we will focus the analysis on critical or defining cases of changes in economic governance, inter-governmental relationships and administrative reform. Thus the design we use draws on analyses of "cases within cases", that is, critical instances such as crises or major reassessments of governance arrangements.

Comparative analysis is a classic research design in political science. The design of such comparative research varies from large-N studies drawing on quantitative methods to comparative case studies emphasizing the explanatory capacity of context (Peters, 2013). The present study is of the latter type; the emphasis is on the contextual and institutional factors that explain if, why, and how a country adopts an international norm of reform concept and integrates it into its domestic governance arrangements. This perspective thus stipulates that rather than comparing three national contexts as such, the comparative approach will only yield results that speak to the broader universe of countries if names proper are replaced by theoretically anchored explanatory variables (compare Przeworski, 1987). In the present analysis we assume that context matters a great deal, that the interplay of institutions and agency typical to a national context can explain variations in the adoption of international norms. Context cannot be distilled into an explanatory variable, or even a cluster of explanatory variables.

Fritz Scharpf has argued along similar lines. He cautions that in research on globalization, "given the multiplicity of—path-dependent—options, it is not surprising that comparative studies may not produce unequivocal findings" (Scharpf, 1998:3) and that "any attempt to explain empirical variation has to take into account the differences in—and contingency of—the explanatory variables" (1998:8). Scharpf's argument could be read as a plea, not for yet another study going after the big numbers and global coverage but rather an analysis of a limited number of in-depth studies on the micro-foundations of globalization; the process through which global or international norms are either translated into domestic reform or rejected by domestic political and administrative officials. That is the theme of this book.

## NOTES

1. The Swedish and Finnish crises in 1991 are among "The Big Five" financial crises listed by Reinhart and Rogoff (2008).
2. Quoted from the WTO's website www.wto.org, accessed January 4, 2013.
3. Asia-Pacific Economic Cooperation.
4. Association of Southeast Asian Nations.
5. Deputy Director, Manufacturing Industries Bureau, Ministry of Economy, Trade and Industry, Japan, October 24, 2005.
6. For an assessment of the state strategy to promote global competitiveness in domestic reform while seeking to shape the international arena, see also Brenner (1999).
7. Ministry of Economy, Trade and Industry. METI, previously called MITI (Ministry of International Trade and Industry) was the key bureaucratic structure coordinating and leading the reconstruction of the Japanese industry after the Second World War and through the booming 1950s and 1960s (Johnson, 1982; Okimoto, 1988; Pierre and Park, 1997).
8. Deputy Director, Manufacturing Industries Bureau, Ministry of Economy, Trade and Industry, Japan, October 24, 2005.

# 3. Still governing the economy? Economic governance

... how wrong it is to assume, as some do, that a strong yen will alleviate the trade balance.
Tadahiro Sekimoto, 1995

## NATION STATES AND THE EMERGING "GLOBAL COMMUNITY"

On November 4, 1994, amid an infected debate between the United States and Japan over the trade imbalance between the two states, Tadahiro Sekimoto, vice chairman of *Keidanren* (Japan Federation of Economic Organizations) and legendary Chairman of NEC, gave a speech before the Foreign Correspondents Club of Japan in Tokyo (*Keidanren Review*, special issue, May 1995). Sekimoto's message, in brief, was that although the yen–dollar exchange rate during the past decade had described a dramatically sloping curve, from ¥255/US dollar in 1984 to ¥115/US dollar in 1994, the trade balance between two countries had remain almost perfectly stable at slightly below $12 billion a year. Therefore, Sekimoto concluded, the root cause of the trade imbalance problem—as well as the policy prescriptions to resolve it—should be sought elsewhere.

Had Sekimoto's analysis ended here, his speech could have been dismissed as a statement presenting the views of one of the negotiating parties in an international trade dispute. But Sekimoto approached the trade imbalance problematic not from the traditional vantage point, countering allegations of unfair competition in the Japanese domestic market with arguments about superior Japanese product quality and only very limited legal trade restrictions. Instead, he looked at these issues from the point of view of the changing nature of economic competition in an era of rapid globalization of national economies. Sekimoto saw the nation state as typical to an economy characterized by an emphasis on institutions and infrastructure. As national economies become increasingly deregulated and less dependent on domestic infrastructural arrangements, nation states as formative structures would be succeeded, first by a "multinational community" and later by what he called a "global community" (*Keidanren Review*, May 1995:4).

Looking at the trade imbalance issue and the causes and consequences of the strong yen in this perspective, the issue becomes less a matter of what macroeconomic policies or regulatory reform Japan ought to pursue to alleviate the trade friction problem and more a question of what political, social, and economic forces determine the competitiveness of national economies and the governance of the domestic economy (see Johnson, 1998:656). This problem, which Paul Krugman (1994a:24) describes as "one of the two great mysteries in economics",[1] has been addressed by a host of political scientists and economists, from Adam Smith onwards (for reviews of this literature, see Kenworthy, 1995; Hall and Soskice, 2001). Also, there is a growing literature on to what extent different institutional arrangements of the state make a difference with regard to national economic competitiveness and, if so, how and why they make a difference (see, e.g. Hall, 1986; Hall and Soskice, 2001; Johnson, 1982; Kenworthy, 1995; North, 1990; Okimoto, 1988; Porter, 1990; Zysman, 1983).

The degree to which international contingencies can alter institutionalized arrangements of domestic economic governance is a critical test of the globalization argument. Globalization is first and foremost an economic project. It aims at removing domestic legal and regulatory obstacles to a free flow of financial and human resources in order to create a more efficient global allocation of resources to boost economic growth. A global economy allocates resources more efficiently than any controlled economic system is able to do and produces an optimal spatial division of labor, based on relative factor costs in different countries. Countries with cheap labor should harbor manufacturing industries while countries with more skilled, but also more costly, labor should specialize in research and knowledge-intensive sectors of the economy.

To facilitate this global market, domestic trade barriers or other protective measures must be removed, hence the WTO's push for deregulated markets within and among countries and the removal of obstacles to overseas penetration of domestic markets. These reforms would take states and markets beyond bilateral trade issues and closer to Sekimoto's envisaged "global community".

Also, in a globalized economy, the economic development of a country is to a high degree a matter of how its main trade partners fare (see Stiglitz, 2003). In a global market-driven division of labor, trade becomes integral to national economies, e.g. in terms of securing raw materials for industry, attracting labor with the necessary skills to develop domestic sources of growth, and to secure export revenues. As the global financial crisis which erupted in August 2008 and subsequent cases of international financial instabilities have made painfully clear, a global deregulation of domestic markets for capital, people, and goods, means that waves of boom and bust travel almost instantly from one country to the next. Domestic economic instability reduces demand on imported goods, thus diffusing the crisis to the country's trading partners.

These developments beg the question of the resilience of domestic institutions in a globalized economy. Governing the economy has historically been one of government's key roles in the advanced capitalist democracies; even classical liberal economists like Adam Smith accorded government a regulatory role in the economy without which markets would not function. From the vantage point of domestic governments, a deregulation of financial and goods markets is a high yield-high risk project, opening up export markets at the same time as it gives overseas companies access to domestic markets (Schaede and Grimes, 2003b).

Thus, even governments who embrace international free trade and a liberalization of capital and financial markets have incentives to maintain some degree of regulatory control over the economy. The ideal scenario is to secure access to markets overseas while domestic markets remain protected from international competition—a strategy which Japan excelled in for several decades after the Second World War—but in order to be a good citizen in the "global community" countries are expected to honor reciprocity.

Providing regulatory frameworks for markets is but the baseline definition of the role of government in the domestic economy and a large number of countries have witnessed their government taking a higher profile in the governance of their economy (Hall and Soskice, 2001; Kenworthy, 1995). Given the centrality of the economy as the source of national wealth—including the public sector's revenues—governments around the world have huge stakes in the growth of the economy and the performance of national industry in international markets. This also applies to almost all other parameters of the economy, such as the level of inflation, unemployment levels, real estate and land prices, and the stability of the financial system.

Governing the economy thus refers to managing a set of complex contingencies while implementing a macroeconomic policy that ensures economic stability and international competitiveness (Hall, 1986). Government has a significant role, or a set of roles, in promoting economic development (Kenworthy, 1995); at the same time there is much to suggest that excessive government *dirigisme* in the economy is counterproductive and could easily end up stifling competition and curtailing economic growth. Another complex contingency relates to the international markets; through skillful domestic policies governments can actively enhance the competitiveness of domestic businesses overseas, but government will also want to keep international champions in the domestic arena and reap parts of the profits they generate.

The impact of globalization on national economies has taken different forms. In some countries, as we discussed in Chapter 2, globalization first emerged in the shape of international speculation against the domestic currency that followed on the deregulation of domestic financial markets. The early 1990s witnessed a series of powerful manifestations of what international financial markets could do to weak currencies. On "Black Wednesday" in the UK in September 1992, the government had to withdraw from ERM cooperation after it had failed to sustain the sterling above the agreed limit (Gamble, 1994). Also in the 1990s Sweden, Korea, Malaysia, Thailand, Indonesia and several other countries experienced aggressive international speculation against their respective currencies (Dennis, 1998; Feldstein, 1998; Johnson, 1998; Lundgren, 1998; Pierre, 1999).

The common scenario in these financial crises has been a national currency pegged either to another currency or to an international currency norm when the government deregulates financial trade barriers, thus exposing the financial market to global speculation. Since the currency has a fixed value rather than one which reflects its true market value, deregulation creates tremendous potential for speculation on whether the national bank can defend the fixed exchange rate. As the historical records in the UK, Sweden, Thailand, Korea, and several other countries testify, defending a fixed currency exchange rate in the face of aggressive international speculation is extremely difficult, if not de facto impossible (Stiglitz, 2003).

Economic governance in a number of countries has also undergone significant reform in the wake of aid and support measures offered by transnational financial institutions like the IMF and, to lesser extent, the World Bank. Donors condition aid on domestic reform towards market liberalization and the termination of monopolized markets. Since national governments prior to the crisis had chosen not to implement such policies, it is fair to assume that these instances represent distinct impositions of norms carried by international organizations on domestic governance arrangements.

These manifestations of a globalized economy have been extremely powerful and difficult for national governments to deal with. However, globalization also evolves in a more subtle and incremental ways and extends over extensive periods of time.

Let us now see the degree to which economic governance in our three case countries has been shaped by international, or bilateral, norms and ideas or whether such governance has been path-dependent and shaped primarily by domestic norms.

## JAPAN

The unparalleled development of the Japanese industry and economy in the post-war period rested to a large extent on the combination of the success of the leading export companies and the capacity of institutions like MITI (and later METI) to withstand international pressures to open up the Japanese domestic markets to international competition. However, by the early 1990s, as Mark Elder (2003:160) observes, "four decades of trade and capital liberalization, however gradual and reluctant, had greatly narrowed the scope for formal protection, and increased foreign scrutiny had made informal protection and administrative guidance more difficult (though not impossible) to hide". Elder's observation is important, for several reasons; economic liberalization was not, as is sometimes suggested, a feature of the 1990s but had a rather long history. From a neo-liberal perspective, wrote Toshio Kamo in 2000, "the present malaise of Japan's economy and of its cities, on the whole is explained as an outcome of the system/policy failures in adjusting to global market standards" (Kamo, 2000:2149). If instead an institutional perspective is adopted, the historical embeddedness of economic and social structure emerges as an explanation for the economic problems. Both perspectives have merit, Kamo concludes; while Japanese society and economy have excelled in conquering export markets they have been less apt at adjusting to the globalization pressures of the 1980s onwards.

Furthermore, the Japanese were incremental in their liberalization since they had strategic interests in protecting their domestic market from overseas competition. Thus, liberalization was not conducted as a response to domestic businesses—rather the opposite—but as incremental concessions to international political and economic pressures. Throughout the post-war period, the Japanese political economy has been shaped by international norms and ideas, particularly of US origin. This dates back to the early post-war occupation regime under General MacArthur but has been present in more subtle forms throughout the decades after the Second World War. Given the importance of export revenues in the post-war Japanese economic recovery, issues related to industrial organization, trade, and market deregulation have been recurrent problems between Japan and key actors in its external environment. This brief analysis on economic governance will focus on these three issues.

## Dismantling the *Keiretsu*

In the early post-war period and US occupation, MacArthur was determined to dismantle the strong integration of Japanese industry. As John Ikenberry notes:

> the economic reform program focused on the dissolving of the *zaibatsu*, the highly concentrated financial and industrial combines that dominated the Japanese economy. In the American view, these giant industrial structures were directly behind both German and Japanese militarism and stood in the way of individual rights and liberties. (Ikenberry, 2007:51)

The *zaibatsu*, and later the *keiretsu*, represented a model of industrial and financial conglomeration which coordinated major companies vertically with subcontractors while at the same time ensuring the provision of investment capital from a bank at the center of the network. The latter aspect of these conglomerates is essential to understanding the logic of the *keiretsu* as Japanese firms traditionally do not have to rely on the stock market to finance investment.

MacArthur would not succeed in his efforts to break the Japanese industrial system. Although the US occupation regime made strong efforts in the late 1940s to dismantle the *zaibatsu* by implementing a system of antitrust laws and other regulations that limited cross-ownership, similar arrangements of highly integrated industrial conglomerates were soon to reappear in the form of *keiretsu*. Cross-ownership, a defining feature of the *keiretsu*, is not, as is usually the case in the West, motivated by a prevention of hostile takeovers but instead serves to express mutual trust and allegiance to a common good.

This arrangement of industrial and financial relationships facilitated long-term industrial planning and continuity in inter-organizational exchanges, thus significantly lowering transaction costs. The *keiretsu* provided a powerful formula for economic growth and were the key industrial vehicles for the "economic miracle" during the post-war decades (Cerny, 2005; Johnson, 1982; Okimoto, 1988). Together with a strong commitment to economic growth and a strong coordinating role by the Ministry of International Trade and Industry (MITI; later METI), the *keiretsu* were integral to the Japanese "developmental state" during the post-war decades (Johnson, 1982).

It was not until well into the 1990s when a series of financial crises hit Japan that the *keiretsu* model of industrial organization would commence its decline. The crisis—a combination of a bursting bubble economy generating huge amounts of capital lost in bad loans and major governance problems in the financial sector (see Amyx, 2004)—prompted the United States, both bilaterally and in concert with the IMF, to insist that the Japanese government reforms its regulatory framework. Removing trade barriers was an obvious target but also deregulating the domestic Japanese more broadly. A decade later, the results of the crisis and the ensuing reform began to emerge. In 2008, David Pilling commented on how the financial turmoil of the 1990s—"the lost decade", as the Japanese tend to call it—had reshaped the Japanese industrial system: "[T]he *keiretsu* system . . . has all but vanished. Cross-shareholdings are about 20 per cent of total equity compared with nearly 50 per cent in the go-go 1980s. Foreign ownership of Japanese shares, just 4.7 per cent in 1990, is above 27 per cent" (Pilling, 2008).

How did this happen? What economic or political force could achieve what a military victory and subsequent occupation had failed to accomplish? Was the dismantling of a model of industrial organization that had proven integral to the Japanese "economic miracle" a logical outcome of the financial crisis of the 1990s? Changing the regulatory framework in order to reduce cross-ownership had a profound and lasting impact on the governance and transformative capacity of Japanese industry. A senior METI official argues in an interview that "after the lift of cross-border transaction regulations and the deregulation of financial markets more broadly, the Japanese culture 'did not work'. This was for instance clear in terms of vertical coordination in the domestic economy. The Japanese economy had an institutionalized practice for reducing output in critical or difficult situations (e.g. reduction in steel production) but this practice was no longer effective or even possible to use after the deregulation."

The "vertical coordination of the domestic economy" which the METI official refers to is the *keiretsu* model of industrial organization. His analysis of the reasons for the reform which caused its decline is clear: "The decision in the 1980s to deregulate cross-border markets was caused by pressures from the United States. This affected trade with steel, textile and semiconductors. The decision was an example of the liberalization ideology which is a defining feature of the 'Washington Consensus'. Japan has a security pact with the United States, and partly for this reason the Japanese government is sensitive to pressures from the US government." Furthermore, the METI official insists that the reform was an imposition of overseas norms which had distinct negative consequences for the Japanese economic system: "The laissez-faire style of the Washington Consensus is not efficient in Asia. Asian culture is very different compared to the US-Anglo culture. The pace of change is slower in the laissez-faire systems compared to countries typical to the Asian culture. The political-economic culture of the Asian countries gives them a better adaptive capacity."[2]

The criticism from the West, particularly the United States, of the *keiretsu* model began in the early post-war period but Japan successfully fended off proposals to terminate those conglomerates for several decades. It was not until Japan found itself in the midst of a severe financial crisis and had to accept assistance from the IMF that the *keiretsu* declined. The Japanese saw little difference between the proposals made bilaterally by the US and the reform program requested by the IMF in the spirit of the Washington Consensus; instead, the difference was that the multilateral rescue package was essential to the Japanese economy and there was therefore little choice but to implement neo-liberal reform.

Later in this chapter we will discuss to what extent the *keiretsu* as a model of industrial organization was set to decline regardless of the financial crisis and the subsequent IMF intervention. As a result of globalization during the 1980s and 1990s, several of the big Japanese export companies in the automobile and electronics industries were gradually transforming themselves from traditional Japanese businesses to global companies, embedded in the markets, industries, and financial systems in strategic export markets. This development posed a major challenge to the *keiretsu* model of corporate coordination. Thus, it is not unlikely that the termination of the *keiretsu* requested by the IMF merely confirmed a process which had already been underway for several years albeit in more subtle forms. *Keiretsu* conglomerates were probably not part of Sekimoto's vision of the "global community".

## Resolving Trade Friction Issues

A result of the successful Japanese economic development during the 1960s and 1970s—the "economic miracle"—was a growing trade surplus with the United States. In the early 1980s, the Americans insisted that the best way to address the issue was to appreciate the value of the yen relative to the dollar. In the 1985 Plaza Accord Japan, West Germany, France, the UK, and the US agreed to collaborate to address trade imbalances, and adjusting currency exchange rates was believed to be a key instrument towards that objective. As a result, the value of the Yen rose rapidly, from ¥242/US dollar in September 1985 to ¥153/US dollar in mid-1986. The appreciation of the yen (*endaka*) had far-reaching consequences for Japanese industry; it drove a process of "hollowing out" of the industry, that is, the relocalization of manufacturing industry from Japan to neighboring countries, primarily China.

Chalmers Johnson (1998:656) argues that the US focus on exchange rates during the 1980s was

> good neoclassical economics but abominable Japanese area studies . . . [the results of tampering with exchange rates] made no difference to the

> trade imbalance, but they stimulated Japan to undertake countermeasures to the high yen, which led to Japan's bubble economy, then to the collapse of the bubble economy, then to Japan's export of its bubble economy to South-East Asia, and finally to the meltdown that confronts us today.

After the Plaza Accord, trade issues between Japan and the United States were handled in a less adversarial fashion. Soon, however, American pressures on Japan increased again. The target now was the extensive regulation of Japanese domestic markets which the US saw as a "structural impediment" to American businesses seeking to enter Japanese markets (Amyx, 2004:135). Japan's response to globalization and economic liberalization had been a combination of maintaining regulatory obstacles to overseas penetration of domestic markets on the one hand, and a strategic exploitation of the opportunities that globalization has offered in terms of access to other countries' markets and international collaboration on the other (Schaede and Grimes, 2003b). Deregulating the Japanese domestic markets therefore became an obvious target for the US negotiators.

## Deregulation

Regulatory reform has potentially widespread ramifications. The dismantling of the *keiretsu* which was discussed earlier was accomplished mainly by changing the regulatory framework so that cross-ownership became much more restricted. Thus changing regulatory frameworks redefines what legal and illegal behavior is in markets.

This observation which holds true in most parts of the world hinges on a couple of assumptions that are often taken for granted. One such assumption is that key exchanges and interactions between the state and the market are, in fact, subject to regulation. Furthermore, even where such rules are implemented, regulatory change will only change behavior as long as rules are enforced. If no rules exist, or if rules are largely ignored, regulatory reform is almost by definition a useless policy instrument. Insisting on domestic deregulation—a common conditionality for assistance from the IMF—will have an impact on formal regulatory frameworks but is not likely to change the conduct of business. Self-regulating or informal governance arrangements are immune to deregulation.

A defining feature of the Japanese political economy is the self-regulation and the informal contacts between industry, finance, and government. The financial system was for a long time coordinated through informal contacts between the Ministry of Finance and the major commercial banks (Amyx, 2004:30). However, a leitmotif in Japan's negotiations with the United States and international financial institutions has been what these parties have seen as excessive domestic regulation in the Japanese economy which was believed to be detrimental to economic development and to overseas competition in domestic Japanese markets. The overseas critique appears however to have been less concerned with the regulatory framework of Japan's economic governance but more targeted at regulations as trade barriers.

Japan's sensitivity towards international norms has to a significant degree been dictated by the performance of its economy. In the early 1990s Japan entered a deep recession which took the remainder of the decade to recover from. The recession was however only the beginning of the economic and financial problems. In November 1997 several key financial institutions collapsed and the bubble economy that had been built up during the past decade burst (Amyx, 2004:182). As a result, Japan was thrown into a deep financial crisis, public budget deficits and debt soared, foreign capital fled the country, and severe cutbacks in public expenditures were implemented. Japan was (once again) urged by the IMF to deregulate its domestic markets. An interviewee comments that "deregulation is a somewhat paradoxical response to the bubble. The bubble was not caused by excessive or inappropriate regulation."[3] To be sure, the governance of the financial system was severely *under*-regulated, a circumstance which, as Amyx's (2004) careful analysis points out, greatly impaired the capacity of the system to address the crisis swiftly and forcefully. It was not until the financial crisis had hit the Japanese economy that regulatory frameworks were put in place to ensure accountability and oversight. Deregulation was not the reform required to address the crisis but the IMF and the US maintained that such reform was necessary.

## Conclusions

Isolating the effects of globalization on the Japanese economy from those triggered by the myriad of other drivers of economic change is a complex task. In the recreation of the Japanese industry after the Second World War, MITI promoted a limited number of industrial sectors and companies to conquer international markets. In the 1990s, when globalization intensified, these companies—NEC, Nissan, Mitsubishi, Toyota and others—had grown into global players with factories and assembly plants in all continents of the world; with credits and loans offered by banks outside Japan; and with little or no need for assistance from METI and perhaps a decreasing inclination to heed its advice. These circumstances suggest that the global diffusion of Japanese industry meant that much of the former predominance of the *keiretsu* model of industrial conglomerates was lost already before the deregulation which the US and the IMF enforced on Japan during the financial crisis.

Assessing the impact of globalization on the Japanese economy is further complicated by the powerful international exchanges orchestrated by the Japanese government. Although strategically logical, it is politically difficult to lament the imposition of overseas norms and philosophies of deregulation when Japanese companies continue to expand their market shares in other countries. Furthermore, Japan has not hesitated to use international institutions for its own purposes when opportunities have arisen. During the 1997 Korean financial crisis, Japan, together with the United States, the World Bank and the IMF, put pressure on Korea to deregulate its domestic markets and allow for Japanese goods to enter Korean markets as part of the IMF support loan (Feldstein, 1998:32). Critics of the Japanese strategy to gain access to Korean markets, one of its main export markets, by piggy-backing on the IMF might even suggest that in doing so it had basically forfeited its right to complain about the IMF's and the World Bank's interference in its own domestic markets.

However, that would be to miss an important point. International pressures on domestic markets and regulatory frameworks as issues in bilateral trade exchanges could be seen as part of the tit-for-tat that comes with engaging in international trade. Those pressures present a different, and more legitimate, kind of external influence than the strings attached to rescue schemes offered by the IMF or the World Bank.

As its key trading partner and military ally, Japan appears to have been consistently anxious to maintain a close dialogue with the United States and to accommodate US interests bilaterally and multilaterally. Throughout most of the post-war period, Japan could prevent that accommodating American political and corporate interests would jeopardize the foundational features of its industrial and financial systems. However, during the financially tumultuous 1990s, Japan had little choice but to implement overseas designed reform programs to a much greater extent than previously in order to secure support from the IMF. This increased both the speed and the range of reform beyond what the Japanese economy and society could accommodate. The result was an increasing "institutional friction" (Steinmo, 2012); reform deviated from entrenched social norms and created uncertainty and confusion. As an interviewee put it, the Japanese model "did not work" any more.

It appears as if US influence on the Japanese economy during the past several decades has gradually become increasingly subtle but, at the same time, more efficient. It has obviously become much less based in formal authority or even military force. Today it draws on changes in the ownership structure of Japanese companies and the insertion of US models of corporate management into Japanese corporate culture (Krauss and Pempel, 2004).

More importantly, the financial crisis during the 1990s enabled the US to shift from a bilateral to a multilateral strategy towards Japan. The IMF's support and aid to Japan to alleviate the crisis became a useful vehicle to promote US trade interests in Japan when bilateral negotiations proved fruitless. As US deputy treasurer Lawrence Summers commented in February, 1998: "In some ways the IMF has done more in these past few months to liberalize these [East Asian] economies and open their markets to United States goods and services than has been achieved in rounds of trade negotiations in the region. And it has done so in serving our critical, short-term and long-term interest" (Summers, 1998; see also Philippi, 2003:288; US Treasury Department, 1998).

In sum, there are clear indications that much of the reform in Japanese economic governance represented a change of reform trajectory and an insertion of overseas norms and values. In some cases, for instance the dismantling of the *keiretsu*, the insertion served to speed up changes that were already underway. Resolving the trade friction issues by appreciating the yen, as Chalmers Johnson argued, made sense from an economic theory point of view but it did not solve the trade deficit problem. Deregulation, finally, had been implemented since the early 1980s but the exposure to international financial institutions in the 1980s triggered deregulation in new sectors which were more strategic to the Japanese economy.

## SWEDEN

Throughout the post-war period, Sweden has for many observers been the epitome of the welfare state. There has been an extensive argument among scholars about the extent to which the welfare state can be politically and economically sustained in a globalized economy. The short answer to the question, coming out of this extensive research, is that there are no clear indications that globalization per se poses a threat to the welfare state (see Chapter 2); "sophisticated statistical analyses fail to pin down with certainty the effects of globalization on the welfare state" (Genschel, 2004:632). Rather, the retrenchments that have been implemented in welfare-state programs over the past couple of decades should be attributed to domestic policy choice and the ascendance of neo-liberal parties to power (Korpi, 2003).

Governing the Swedish economy during the emergence of globalization in the 1980s and 1990s could in some respects be thought of as the ultimate governance challenge. Sweden at that time had most of the political, economic, and institutional features that were believed to be incompatible with globalization; a big public sector; high tax levels and a progressive tax scale; redistributive policies; an advanced system of corporatist involvement in policy and implementation; autonomous agencies; fiscal and budgetary instability; and a highly regulated labor market.

The early post-war decades had seen Sweden build a prosperous society, sustained by continued high levels of economic growth and the development of a welfare state. This arrangement was promoted by a regime featuring a centralized industrial community, strong unions, and a Social Democratic government. The Social Democrats dominated the political scene throughout much of the post-war period as a party in government 1932–1976, 1982–1991, and 1994–2006. Since the 2006 elections Sweden is governed by a non-socialist coalition government dominated by the neo-liberal Moderate Party.

The political economy of the Swedish welfare state rested on a high level of income tax, universal entitlements, moderate levels of corporate taxes, and a redistribution of wealth through the public sector. In addition, strong interest organizations promoted and protected social constituencies. The welfare state depended on export revenues and government sought to find the political and economic sweet spot between taxation and regulation on the one hand and not interfering with the leading export-oriented sectors of the economy on the other. This was the essence of the "mixed economy" where industrial capitalism existed alongside extensive public programs of welfare provision and redistribution.

The model began to crumble in the 1970s when tax fatigue set in and there were growing sentiments towards individualism and freedom of choice instead of having the state providing services from the cradle to the grave at a high cost. For the first time in more than four decades the Social Democrats were placed in opposition in 1976 and a coalition of non-socialist parties took over government.

In terms of economic policy and governance the real change began in the early 1990s when taxes were gradually cut, market-based alternatives in service delivery emerged, and an overall reassessment of the difficult question of taxes versus services took place in government and in all the major political parties. Equally important, economic governance was centralized to the Department of Finance and budgetary and fiscal discipline was given top priority.

Twenty years later the result of these changes in policy and governance is easy to see. Between 1993 and 2012 economic growth has been higher than among the EU countries; public spending as a percentage of GDP has dropped from 67 percent to 49 percent; public debt is down from 70 to 37 percent of the GDP; and a budget deficit of 11 percent has been replaced by a surplus of 0.3 percent (*The Economist*, 2013). The international business press is praising this economic turnaround. *Financial Times* named Anders Borg the best finance minister in Europe and *The Economist*, a journal not known for its leftist leanings, suggests that Milton Friedman would feel ideologically more at home in any of the Scandinavian countries than in Washington, DC.

This dramatic change of trajectory appears to have all the features of adapting the domestic economy to a globalizing economy. The change in policy and governance was driven by both short-term and more long-term factors. The acute manifestation of globalization was the deep financial crisis that hit Sweden in the autumn of 1991. The crisis punctuated the equilibrium that had characterized economic policy and governance through much of the post-war period and defined a new "path" which Sweden has since pursued. In addition, Sweden has extensive experience of coping with international contingencies and volatile export markets.

It would also be tempting to attribute the profound policy change to the ascendance of non-socialist parties to government. The post-1991 model of economic governance has however been supported and implemented by both sides of the political aisle. Thus, the core features of the economic policy and governance of the 1990s and 2000s—budgetary and fiscal control; increasing centrality of the Department of Finance; rigorous attention to key parameters of the economy such as inflation, debt, and unemployment and conforming to the EU macroeconomic criteria—has not stirred political conflict. To be sure, the political elites in Sweden seem to agree that consensus is essential in the adaptation to changes in the external environment because it implies a long-term vision and provides the business community with regulatory stability.

Another potential explanation for the successful change of economic policy is related to the decline of corporatism. This model of interest representation has proven to be an efficient model of governance in accommodating change and responding to international economic pressure (Katzenstein, 1984, 1985). Given its emphasis on distributive policies, it has fared less well in political economies where budgetary control is a top political priority and exogenous institutions define the key parameters of the economy, which is the context Sweden entered in the 1990s.

Our conclusion thus far is that the change in macroeconomic policy and governance in the early 1990s should be attributed to the financial crisis which showed the forces of overseas speculation against the domestic currency. The political and institutional outcome of the crisis provided tighter control over the economy, emphasizing the importance of budgetary balance. Also, Sweden joining the EU in 1996 introduced a set of macroeconomic criteria which effectively prevented distributive excesses.

Let us now investigate in some more detail how these international pressures were accommodated in the economic governance.

## The 1992 Currency Crisis

This crisis did not emerge as lightning from clear skies. The Swedish financial system had been in turbulence during the latter part of the

1980s. A deregulation of credit markets in 1985 contributed to a bubble economy during the 1980s which sent the major commercial banks into a crisis in 1990 (see Englund, 1999).[4] Furthermore, the deregulation of the currency market in 1989 significantly reduced the capacity of the national bank (*Riksbanken*) to monitor or control the flow of currency across Sweden's borders (Telasuo, 2000). The state came to the rescue of the banks but the financial system and currency market remained volatile, as was indeed the case in much of Europe at that time.

Sweden had a history of a country with high inflation and a tendency to use devaluation as a means of adjusting its price levels to that of other countries. International and domestic financial markets doubted that the *Riksbanken* would be able to defend a fixed exchange rate and began speculating that they would have to float the krona which was pegged to an international currency norm. After a period of intense struggle to fend off speculation, the *Riksbank* decided on November 19, 1992 to float the currency (for detailed accounts of the development of the crisis, see Englund, 1999; Dennis, 1998; Hinnfors and Pierre, 1998; Lundgren, 1998; Pierre, 1999).

As discussed in the previous chapter, the political elite perceived this aggressive speculation against the krona as a powerful manifestation of a global, deregulated market. Again, the political elite were taken complete aback by the currency crisis in 1992. It had not seen the crisis coming, despite the instabilities in the financial system; despite differences in rent levels between Sweden and other countries; and despite the deregulation, the instabilities in the credit system, and the overheated real estate market. Furthermore, a major tax reform implemented in 1990 and 1991—referred to as "the tax reform of the century"—capped the marginal income tax rate at 50 percent. The reform meant that tax deductions for interest rates lost some of their value which made real estate investment less attractive and may have helped burst the "bubble" in the real estate market. In retrospect, senior representatives for the major political parties agree that the sequencing of tax reform and the 1985 deregulation of the credit markets was not sound economic policy (Pierre, 1999; on sequencing of reform, see Frenkel, 2003).

The crisis set economic development in Sweden back for several years. GDP fell by 6 percent between 1991 and 1993, unemployment reached double-digit levels, and the public sector went through severe cutbacks. Thus, the crisis which followed on a decade or more of gradually deteriorating economic performance and instabilities showed at a glance the importance of budgetary discipline in a deregulated, globalizing economy. It is safe to say that this was a "formative moment" in macroeconomic policy and governance which provided momentum for extensive reform. Government spent much of the remainder of the 1990s restoring public finances.

## Joining the EU

The financial crisis and its aftermath coincided with Sweden moving closer to Europe; the country applied for membership in the EU in 1991 and joined the Union in 1996.[5] The EU defines a set of criteria (the so-called Maastricht criteria) which guide the macroeconomic policy of the member states: the budget deficit must not exceed 30 percent of the GDP; the gross national debt is capped at 60 percent of the GDP; and inflation should not exceed 1.5 percent of the average inflation of the three member states with the lowest inflation. These criteria thus define fairly strict macroeconomic parameters for the member states and were probably helpful in implementing a tighter budgetary regime.

The EU membership is a very different matter from managing a short-term financial crisis. Embedding the country politically and economically in an extensive regional effort of economic and political integration is an unprecedented step towards international integration for the politically and militarily non-committed Sweden. Translating international norms into domestic rules, or indeed transferring large parts of domestic regulatory capacity to transnational institutions, has been a major task for the Swedish bureaucracy since Sweden joined the EU (Jacobsson and Sundström, 2006). Conforming to these international norms should not be seen as an exogenous imposition on domestic autonomy, partly because Sweden actively sought membership in the Union and partly because transnational norms are generated from within a democratic system in which Sweden is an active partner and participant. The EU is a good example of regional cooperation to promote collective goals related to growth and security, but as with all such arrangements their success is contingent on the submission of its member states to collective decisions (Schmidt, 1999).

To sum up, Sweden's first encounter with the deregulated global economy uncovered the structural problems and imbalances in the economy. Although this was not a case of importing international norms, the 1991 financial crisis certainly drove home the magnitude of speculation against the nation's currency and the importance of managing the economy so that exposure to future speculation was to be minimized. The EU membership, on the other hand, has all the ingredients of integrating international norms into the domestic regulatory system. A growing part of rule making which pertains to Sweden is in fact not conducted in Sweden but in Brussels. Interestingly, the EU membership and the loss of autonomy it entails is almost never related to internationalization or globalization in Swedish political discourse.

## THE UNITED STATES

If Japan and Sweden have experienced the challenges that international institutions or global investment capital can present to national governments, the United States observed the emerging globalization from a slightly different vantage point. There are four circumstances in particular that set the US apart from Japan and Sweden, and indeed all the advanced industrial democracies.

First, American businesses and the US government are embedded in a significantly bigger domestic market than Japan or Sweden. We saw in Chapter 1 that the United States trade dependency during the early 2000s is at about the same level as Japan. If we extend the time series back to the 1980s, however, Japan had a trade-to-GDP-ratio hovering around 25 percent while the same statistics for the US were below 20 percent (Sweden, by comparison, at that time was above 60 percent). Businesses in industrial economies with low trade dependency can thus sell their products domestically; their prices are less (if at all) tied to overseas competitors; and fluctuations in overseas markets do not impact the industry. A strong domestic market and low trade dependency thus protect and cushion domestic businesses and reduce the level of uncertainty for both businesses and government. This is not to say that US markets have been "closed shops", only that low trade dependency means fewer contingencies to deal with.

The strength of global pressures on domestic markets is also closely related to the configuration of those markets. Industrial economies are more susceptible to global competition than economies with a large service sector. Automobiles or furniture can be manufactured basically anywhere but service-sector businesses are typically localized. The global impact on the growing US service sector has been much more indirect and moderate compared to the industrial sector. The gradual transformation of an industrial economy towards a service-sector based economy thus reduces the economy's exposure to globalization. Eisner (2000:222) makes this point with specific reference to the United States: "many exaggerate the potential extent of globalization because they fail to recognize that the U.S. has a service-based economy. While some services can be traded internationally . . . most services are locally oriented".

Second, the United States has experienced less ideological "friction" between the global free trade regime and its domestic macroeconomic and regulatory policy style. If Japan and perhaps even more so Sweden have had problems embracing the virtue of small government, deregulation, and catering to global investors, the United States has traditionally had a far more market-embracing political approach (see Campbell et al., 1991; Madrick, 2009; Spulber, 1995). True, different Presidential administrations have viewed these matters slightly differently, in part owing to the nature of the issues they were addressing, but public policy overall in the US is more favorable towards the market and more averse to interventions in the market than is the case in Japan or Sweden.

Third and related to the previous point, economic governance in the United States differs in several important aspects from that of Japan or Sweden. While these latter countries have had a long history of more state-centric governance arrangements in their economies, economic governance in the United States is best understood at the level of industries or industrial sectors (Campbell et al., 1991). Economic governance is also to a very large extent a self-regulating process; it is intriguing to note that in the typology of a total of 23 economic governance mechanisms outlined by Campbell et al. (1991:14), none is executed by government institutions. Federal government has not been inclined to launch a comprehensive policy towards industry, as has been the case in Japan and Sweden and a large number of other industrial democracies. That said, the federal government plays important roles for economic development and structural transformation both in conventional terms, for example through macroeconomic policy and regulatory frameworks towards the market, and also through its R&D and defense spending. Indeed, as was pointed out earlier, these roles could easily amount to programs that in many other countries are seen as important elements of an industrial policy (Graham, 1992; Nester, 1997).

The fourth and final feature of the United States during globalization is that it has been significantly more influential on the policies promoted by international financial institutions than have most other countries. The US has an effective veto power over major decisions by the IMF and the World Bank. The previously discussed Washington Consensus has assisted the US in pursuing its interests overseas, particularly with regard to opening up domestic markets in recipient countries to foreign competition. At the same time, the US has successfully protected its own key domestic markets, for example the agricultural markets, from competition from developing countries (Stiglitz, 2003). Thus, if Japan excelled in "permeable insulation" (Schaede and Grimes, 2003b) during its high growth period, the United States, too, has successfully combined protection of domestic markets with influencing international institutions.

Taken together, these features of the American political economy suggest that the US has been less exposed to international norms that deviate from those implemented by domestic institutions than most other countries. Instead, the United States has been a forerunner in advocating free trade and the abolition of domestic barriers to trade; in other words, America has been a transmitter of the international norms that define economic globalization more than it has been a recipient of such norms. This means that the United States has had far fewer problems in adapting to the globalizing economy; globalization as shorthand for deregulated financial markets and free trade has been actively promoted by the United States and conforms to a high degree to its domestic regulatory arrangements.

That having been said, it is of course also true that the US economy has not been untouched by global economic change. As a mature industrial economy subscribing to the idea of free trade the US has been exposed to competition from countries with lower production costs, not least the Asian economies. At some instances, the US has introduced import tariffs to protect the domestic industry. In the early 2000s the George W. Bush administration introduced import tariffs on steel. The WTO ruled that tariffs were in violation of free trade and the US subsequently eliminated the tariffs (Hytrek and Zentgraf, 2008:62).

## NAFTA

Regional cooperation, as we have seen in the cases of Japan and Sweden, has been a common strategy to protect the domestic economy from global economic pressures. As we also pointed out earlier, the efficiency of such cooperative strategies hinges on the commitment of the partnering countries to the collective project. Somewhat paradoxically, such commitments to regional projects may often be seen as manifestations of globalization and less as a response to globalization. In the United States, one of the perhaps more ostentatious manifestations of economic globalization and its (domestic and regional) responses in the United States has been the emergence of the North American free trade agreement (NAFTA), signed in December, 1992 (Hufbauer and Schott, 1993). The United States and Canada already had a free-trade agreement and the 1992 accord brought Mexico into the free-trade zone. Critics of NAFTA argued that it would mean that tens of thousands of American jobs would be relocated to Mexico where labor costs are lower. Special interest groups in Washington, DC sought, often successfully, to protect their interests by insisting on compensation or protection. The advocates of the deal, on the other hand, argued that the jobs that would move to Mexico were coming from declining sectors of the economy with little prospect of surviving in the global economy. More importantly, they argued, the arrangement would give US businesses access to the buoyant Mexican market, creating a large number of jobs in the United States.

NAFTA had been negotiated by the George Bush, Sr. administration and was inherited by the Clinton administration after the 1992 Presidential election. Clinton was just as strong a supporter of the free-trade arrangement as his predecessor and invested much political clout to ensure passage of the deal in Congress. His first inaugural speech, delivered in January 1993, was devoted to instilling faith in embracing change and "renewal" among the American people. The speech could well be seen as a first step towards securing passage of the NAFTA deal in Congress, which was one of the Clinton administration's biggest challenges in 1993.[6] NAFTA entailed provisions in two areas that were particularly sensitive to the US; the protection and compensation of labor and the enforcement of environmental standards. George Bush stated very early in the discussions on NAFTA that there would be provisions to compensate dislocated US workers and to ensure that labor rights were upheld in the accord.[7]

The issue we need concern ourselves with here is not so much whether the outcomes of the agreement have been successful in terms of trade volumes or to what extent the net change of American jobs turned out to be positive or negative. Instead, NAFTA and the process of its domestic accommodation raise two questions about the impact of globalization manifested in the dismantling of regional trade barriers.

One issue is related to globalization and domestic structural change. The key challenge in this debate to both the scholars and the politicians and, indeed, to the concerned citizen, is to distinguish structural transformation caused by globalization from the type of structural change which is indigenous to a capitalist economy. The history of industrial capitalism is the history of jobs lost in declining and uncompetitive sectors and new jobs created in emerging and competitive sectors. Globalization has removed domestic protective measures and thus increased the pace of structural transformation.

While it is clear that a large number of jobs have left the United States through these processes, this development does not strike the international observer as abnormal to the trajectory of structural change of an advanced economy. Indeed, as an OECD report on the US economy noted in 2005, "the frequently cited estimate of 3.3 million white-collar jobs moving overseas by 2015 translates into an average quarterly job-loss rate of 55 000 jobs, which is small in comparison to the more than 7 million jobs destroyed on average every quarter as a result of the normal functioning of the economy" (OECD, 2005:7). The OECD concludes that globalization has not affected the US manufacturing industry to any exceptional degree. If anything, they argue, globalization has helped set in motion processes of industrial restructuring which are essentially good for the economy.

The second issue is related to the accommodation of international economic pressure and regional accords to contain such pressures. Governments in most countries play an important role in mitigating the social and economic impact of the structural transformation, although less so in the United States compared to for instance European countries. The strategy chosen by the Bush and Clinton administrations was to secure NAFTA and to compensate domestic constituencies that were negatively affected by the economic change triggered by the expansion of the free-trade area. Labor, as mentioned, was one such constituency. One of the reasons why American labor has been such a powerful critic of trade liberalization, John Ruggie (1998) suggests, is that government spends much less on labor market policy programs like training compared to its international competitors. Preparing for, and assisting domestic labor in, structural changes in the economy by offering training, unemployment insurance, and a social safety net to ease the process of transferring from one job to the other could be seen as an important instrument in global economic competition.

Again, globalization has increased the speed of domestic economic transformation and the smoother the process of adapting labor to new jobs in emerging industries the easier the economy as a whole adapts to changes in the global economy. NAFTA brought these issues to the fore in the American debate on the transformation of the economy.

**Deregulating Financial Markets**

In international negotiations, the United States tends to be a strong advocate of deregulation of domestic markets and in that respect America practices what it preaches. Beginning in the 1970s but gaining significant momentum during the Reagan administration in the1980s, the US has implemented extensive deregulation reform in a number of sectors of the economy, such as transport, communication, and energy.

In the 1990s, important regulatory changes were implemented in the US financial system. Perhaps the most significant reform came in 1999 when the Glass Steagall Act from 1933 was repealed. The Glass Steagall Act separated commercial banks, investment banks, and insurance companies. Removing these barriers may have contributed to the 2008 financial crisis since it facilitated increasing risk in loan giving, for instance sub-prime loans, which caused the dramatic slump in large parts of the US real estate market in the mid-2000s. Altman (2009a:2) argues however that the root cause of the crisis was not the repeal of the Glass Steagall Act but instead the "invariably lethal combination" of "very low interest rates and unprecedented levels of liquidity". Either way, the dramatic loss of real estate value led to the collapse and government bailout of the Federal National Mortgage Association (FNMA, nickname Fannie Mae) and the

Federal Home Loan Mortgage Corporation (FHLMC, or Freddie Mac). At that time, the financial system was beginning to destabilize and the full crisis came in August 2008.

The process leading up to the 2007 sub-prime crisis and the 2008 financial crisis is extremely complex and technical. For the present analysis our main concern is whether deregulation was implemented in response to global pressures or as a strategy to boost international competitiveness. The available accounts of the crisis provide no evidence of any international or global pressures driving the deregulation that may have helped cause the crisis.

Since national financial systems are increasingly integrated, the crises in the US financial system spread across the world, causing a world-wide recession. In the US, the Obama administration committed itself to introduce regulation to prevent a similar crisis from happening again. During the 2012 Presidential election campaign Obama accused Republican candidate Mitt Romney for suggesting tax cuts that would jeopardize once again the stability of the financial system. On both sides of the aisle there seems to be quite moderate interest in introducing additional and more restrictive regulation of the financial system.

## Concluding Comments

The United States has been a dominant player in world politics throughout the post-war period and most markedly so after the fall of the Berlin Wall. In terms of economic globalization the twentieth century has in many ways been "the American century" with a global diffusion of American products, military presence, and lifestyle. American economic governance, characterized by a much more limited political presence than in countries like Japan or Sweden, was shaped by endogenous preferences and institutional arrangements.

Extending the free-trade zone in North America placed issues of domestic accommodation and compensation in the face of globalization on the US political agenda. These measures, for instance the TAA programs created to support dislocated workers, appear to have been typically ad hoc and did not signal first steps towards a more general economic strategy in a globalized economy. The sheer size of the US economy and domestic market coupled with a lower political or public presence in the market protect the market both from extensive penetration by overseas businesses and also from extensive political interference in the market. Globalization has thus had a very limited influence indeed on economic governance in the United States, at the same time as it has been the symbol of the global presence of American political and economic interests.

## CONCLUDING DISCUSSION

The three countries selected for this study have historically built much of their wealth from export revenues. This applies particularly to Japan and Sweden where domestic markets are insufficient to allow for the economy of scale required for industrial capitalism. However, US exports contributed significantly to the success of American industrialism during the past century (Eckes and Zeiler, 2003; Spulber, 1995). Thus, we need to look beyond trade as a fraction of GDP to understand the economic dominance of the US; American export revenues represent a smaller percentage of the US GDP than corresponding statistics for Japan and Sweden but US exports in volume is bigger than that for the other countries. This means that the United States can be a truly global economic player without at the same time feeling the pressures of globalization at home.

Japan and Sweden present a more dynamic strategy towards their external environments. Both subscribe to the idea of free trade since they are highly dependent on export revenues. At the same time, developing globally competitive companies requires to some extent protected domestic markets that can foster such businesses. Both countries thus had extensive experience with complex international contingencies long before globalization emerged. Their systems of economic governance were more susceptible to international pressures than the US financial system. In Japan, the institutionalized model of industrial organization and its awkward informal and under-regulated financial system came under severe international pressure during the financial crisis. Similarly in Sweden the failure to anticipate how deregulated financial and currency markets could be used for speculation against the currency caused a deep financial crisis. In both cases it is easy to see the impact of globalization manifested either bilaterally, multilaterally or by an anonymous "market".

Thus the three countries tell different stories about their experiences with globalization. While all three countries have extensive experience in pursuing their interests overseas, Japan has had the biggest challenges in coping with global pressures, particularly during and after the financial crisis in the 1990s. Sweden has kept a low international profile, emphasizing collective action in political and economic arenas, and loyally implementing (if not over-implementing; see Zannakis, 2009) international agreements. Meanwhile, Swedish governments of all ideological orientations have underscored the importance of fostering globally competitive business and research sectors. The United States, finally, has used bilateral and multilateral strategies to unlock foreign, regulated markets while at the same time having been relatively protected domestically. It is true, of course, that several US industrial sectors (e.g. textile, steel, automobile) were severely hit by international competition during the 1960s, 1970s, and 1980s, but these were more manifestations of changing terms of trade and competitive advantages than of a truly globalized economy.

It is worth noting that all three countries have seen regional economic collaboration as an important component of their adjustment to globalization. The EU represents the most advanced example of integration in this respect. NAFTA is a free-trade agreement with very limited governance arrangements. ASEAN, finally, emerged as a free-trade framework but seems intent on developing regional governance structures.

## NOTES

1. The other "mystery" is what determines the cyclical pattern of boom and recession in the economy.
2. Senior official, Manufacturing Industries Bureau, Ministry of Economy, Trade and Industry, October 24, 2005.
3. Senior official, Manufacturing Industries Bureau, Ministry of Economy, Trade and Industry, October 24, 2005. See also Stiglitz, 2003.
4. Englund (1999) argues that while the deregulation in 1985 may have contributed to the "bubble" it was not the sole cause of the "bubble" or the subsequent crisis in the financial system.
5. Sweden has (so far) chosen not to join the Eurozone and has thus to some extent been able to avoid the ramifications of the Euro crisis in several Southern European countries.
6. For a detailed account of the negotiations leading up to NAFTA, see Cameron and Tomlin (2000).
7. Issues related to the enforcement of environmental standards were regulated in a separate accord, the North American Agreement on Environmental Cooperation (NAAEC) (see Johnson and Beaulieu, 1996).

# 4. Cities and regions in a globalized world: inter-governmental relationships

> If we are to be one nation in any respect, it clearly ought to be in respect to other nations.
>
> James Madison, *The Federalist* (1788; quoted in Bilder 1989:821)

## RESCALING PUBLIC AUTHORITY: CITIES AS "ARCHITECTS OF GLOBALIZATION"

The era of globalization is said to be the era of cities and regions. As globalization progresses it "rescales" domestic institutional hierarchies in which cities and regions are conventionally seen as subordinate structures with little choice but to implement central government decisions, and opens up new arenas for subnational government to pursue their interests (see Brenner, 2004; Pierre, 2011b). Indeed, globalization is often said to be localized in cities and regions more than nation states. Urban and regional elites have become what Susan Clarke (2006:56) calls the "key architects of globalization".

In a similar vein, Saskia Sassen points out that "national and global markets . . . require central places where the work of globalization gets done" (Sassen, 2000:81). Globalization, according to Sassen, is localized in "global cities" hosting global financial and institutional actors where corporate headquarters, up-scale housing and "world-class culture" share the urban space with immigrants and the urban underclass (Sassen, 1991, 1996). Thus, globalization impinges on cities in a number of different ways; as an arena, as an opportunity structure, and as a major adaptive challenge (see Alger, 1998, 2010; Beauregard, 1995; Bilder, 1989; Brenner, 1999; Goetz and Clarke, 1993; Hambleton and Simone Gross, 2007; Keil, 1998; Sellers, 2001).

The rescaling of political authority that is associated with globalization refers to the process whereby cities and regions challenge the domestic institutional hierarchy and position themselves as international actors, forming their own networks, and selecting strategic partners overseas, independently of the state (Brenner, 1999, 2004; van der Heiden, 2010). The conventional institutional hierarchy and the distribution of authority it represents is replaced by a multi-level contextualized and negotiated institutional order in which agency transgresses institutional boundaries (Bache and Flinders, 2004; Brenner, 1999, 2004; Hooghe and Marks, 2003; Piattoni, 2010). Rescaling is a consequence of a more permeable distinction between the domestic and the global. Cities and regions in the globalizing landscape are less constrained by the domestic institutional hierarchy and seek strategic partnerships on a global level.

As the "architects of globalization", then, cities and regions are both targets and drivers of globalization. Their strategies bypass the domestic institutional hierarchy and aim at building or joining international networks. Some of this is done with an approving nod or even encouragement from central government whereas in other cases it is tolerated more than supported (Fry, 2013; van der Heiden, 2010).

This chapter explores two competing hypotheses concerning the impact of globalization. According to one hypothesis, globalization has led to greater similarities among cities in different national contexts. This should manifest itself in a high degree of similarity among Japanese, US, and Swedish cities with regard to the challenges they are facing and the strategies they employ to tackle those challenges. The competing hypothesis states that cities respond to globalization challenges in ways which are path-dependent to the national context in which they are embedded.

The focus of our analysis is strictly on governance. Accordingly, the key questions we ask are to what extent there are patterns of increasing uniformity in urban internationalization in different types of national contexts, that is, is subnational internationalization a global phenomenon? To what extent do different nation–state institutional arrangements encourage or prevent urban and regional internationalization? In short; does the pattern and extent of internationalization of local and regional government lend support to the globalization hypothesis, or does it instead suggest that there are important differences in the extent and meaning of subnational internationalization in Japan, Sweden and the United States?

The chapter first looks at international organizations and networks for subnational government, since cities and regions frequently choose to pursue internationalization multilaterally rather than bilaterally. We then discuss rescaling and the changing balance between state, region, and city in more empirical detail in order to uncover the causes and drivers of subnational internationalization. The third section is devoted to empirical analysis which proceeds in two parts. It first reports a quantitative, comparative analysis of urban governance and subnational internationalization in Japan, Sweden, and the United States. We then report the in-depth case studies on these three countries. The chapter draws to some extent on a questionnaire study conducted among local authorities in Japan, Sweden, and the United States in 2006.[1]

## CITIES AND REGIONS AS COLLECTIVE ACTORS

In spite of the fact that cities compete for private investment and attention from the nation state, subnational government has a long history of national and international collaboration to pursue common interests. At the national level, national associations of local authorities can be found in 115 countries (Lidström, 2011). Some of these associations include both local and regional government.

Cities are also active in international organizations. The "United Cities and Local Governments" (UCLG), headquartered in Barcelona, is devoted to the pursuit of a broad policy agenda and has more than 1000 cities as members. UCLG was created in 2004 as a merger of IULA ("International Union of Local Authorities"), formed already in 1913, and the United Towns Organization (UTO). Equally important, the ICLEI, "Local Governments for Sustainablity" which pursues a more focused agenda, also counts some 1000 members.

In the EU, cities act collectively in several different networks and organizations, for instance the Eurocities network, set up by six cities in 1986 but today hosting 130 members; Eurotowns, created in 1991 to organize medium-sized cities; and the Council of European Municipalities and Regions (CEMR), created already in 1951. The

CEMR works mainly as a lobby organization in Brussels. These organizations, in turn, frequently set up task-specific groups on a variety of issues. In addition, there are a number of more specialized networks for cities in the Union, e.g. the "Polis" network which is a forum for the management of public transport issues or "Reves" which brings together cities and regions with an interest in "social economy".

International organizations for local authorities have thus been in existence for a century. Some organizations are created mainly to facilitate cultural or other forms of exchange whereas other networks, particularly in the EU, serve as lobby organizations. It is fair to assume, however, that globalization and the professionalization of local government in the developed world have contributed to giving these organizations a more important role as forums for exchanging ideas and experiences. The fact that cities commit extensive time and money to their involvement in these international organizations and networks is proof of the significance of these structures in disseminating knowledge and expertise among local authorities.

In addition to membership in national and international organizations, cities increasingly form partnerships or smaller networks with cities in other countries. Previously, these partnerships, for example sister cities, were created to facilitate cultural exchange in various forms. More recently, these partnerships are predominantly defined by strategic considerations. As a senior official in the Swedish Association of Local Authorities and Regions (SALAR) put it: "Folk dancing in the city square is a thing of the past".[2] The past couple of decades have seen a growth and reorientation of cities and regions in international arenas and transnational networks to disseminate information and expertise, and to "forge norms about the nature and terms of particular issues" (Betsill and Buckeley, 2004:472). Among the issues that have been deemed appropriate for transnational networks of cities, there has been particular interest in climate change and sustainable development as components of global environmental governance (Alger, 2010; Betsill and Buckeley, 2004).

Again, these international networks have developed largely with central government as a passive bystander in all three countries. However, the Japanese central government has been actively encouraging subnational internationalization, particularly in the late 1980s and early 1990s along with the "hollowing out" and relocalization of Japanese businesses. The US Constitution, Article II, Section 2 states that only the president can sign treaties with foreign nations but several states and cities have signed accords or agreements with regions or cities overseas (see Fry, 1998, 2013; Fry et al., 1989). This is also the case for the large number of cities who, in addition to joining international networks for cities or regions, also pursue bilateral forms of collaboration (see Aldecoa and Keating, 1999).

The institutional forms and purposes of national and international collaboration among cities have thus changed considerably over the past few decades. While global networks and organizations have existed for several decades, if not a century, and thus cannot be causally related to globalization, the more recent patterns of strategic cooperation resonate with several processes which can be attributed to globalization. Budgetary cutbacks coupled with a policy emphasizing urban and regional self-reliance have prompted cities and regions to create strategic networks overseas. As we will see later, however, there is significant variation both within and among the three countries in this respect.

Thus, international initiatives by cities and regions may be driven less by globalization as such and more by the domestic adaptation to globalization. The difference is not altogether academic as globalization implies a structural pressure whereas adaptation implies some degree of choice. Some of these international initiatives seek to insert the city or region into an international network or organization. In other instances, internationalization is conducted as bilateral exchanges, or with groups of local authorities coordinating their efforts to build contacts overseas. Cities and regions display, as we will see later in this chapter, a wide variety of internationalization strategies owing to what they seek to achieve.

## STATES, REGIONS, CITIES, AND GLOBALIZATION: THE CHANGING INSTITUTIONAL BALANCE

Globalization has impacted inter-governmental relationships in the advanced Western democracies through complex processes. The main drivers of such reform have not been globalization per se but rather the adaptation strategies implemented by central government. In order to boost national competitiveness, central government cut back on its expenditures, including subsidies to local and regional government.

Furthermore, central government in many countries advanced the notion that the success of cities in a globalizing world depends on the competitiveness of cities and drove home the idea that cities and regions must develop according to their preconditions (Brotchie et al., 1995; Buck et al., 2005; Johansson, 1991). The subtext to this policy was that cities could no longer rely on the state to provide a safety net or protection against global markets and that cities and regions must be prepared to accept greater responsibility for their future prosperity. It was also a policy which diffused the model of the public sector as a critical component in national competitiveness from the national to the subnational levels of government.

Obviously, this rather distinct change in the relations among central, regional, and local institutions had ramifications for local and regional governance. This was part of central government's reform strategy; it had emphasized reform at the regional and local levels towards more inclusive and collaborative forms of governance. If subnational government was going to be able to continue to deliver good public service with a tighter budget it would have to engage societal partners and devise collaborative strategies.

This shift from a hierarchical and functional towards a territorial governance arrangement was intended to shape not only public service delivery but also the role of cities and regions in economic development; they would have less support from the state than previously but also enjoy more discretion and latitude in forming governance in their jurisdiction. True, the basic rationale of subnational government is to provide territorial rather than functional or sectoral governance, but reform in inter-governmental relationships during the 1980s and 1990s incentivized cities and regions to further mobilize resources in its territory and to invite all key players in their territory into the process of governance.

The new model of inter-governmental relationships had consequences for the capacity of institutions at different levels to accommodate global economic pressures. Central government, not least in Europe, mitigated for a long period of time the impact of international competition on local economies (see, e.g. Knox and Taylor, 1995). However, when nation states devised a neo-liberal formula to enhance its competitiveness in the globalizing economy, that mitigating role was largely dismantled. Subnational governments and their business community were now more exposed to global economic pressure.

The good news, some might say, is that cities and regions probably have more experience in dealing with contingencies than do nation states. Subnational government has been more immediately exposed to economic restructuring than the state where a decline in one sector of the economy to some extent is balanced by growth in other sectors. There are also institutional explanations for this pattern; cities have also had the state as a powerful external actor to relate to. State–local relations in many countries, for example the UK and USA, are characterized by limited local autonomy, hence local government have little choice but to abide by central government directives (King and Pierre, 1990). This means, as Peter Marcuse and Ronald van Kempen (2000:262) argue, that "globalization . . . is only one of the forces determining the spatial pattern of cities, and a force not coming into play for the first time in the recent period. It must be seen as an extension of forces already present over a much longer period of time."

Globalization impacts government at different institutional levels differently and those governments have different experiences in relating to a volatile environment. For the nation state, globalization introduced a new and powerful external actor—the deregulated international investment capital—and governments struggled to learn what this new situation meant and how to manage its economy in order to protect themselves from the forces of global capital. Cities and regions, on the other hand, were familiar with the awesome ramifications of economic and industrial restructuring but their strategic options were few since their capacity to alter their economic structure was quite limited.

Furthermore, some cities and regions are more exposed to international pressures than others, just as some are more inclined to embark on a strategy of internationalization and forging cross-border partnerships than others. Much of this has to do with economic structure, size, and local or regional entrepreneurship. As we will see later, cities (even within the same country) take rather different views on internationalization. Rescaling is thus not a structural imperative; it provides subnational actors with an opportunity structure which they may or may not choose to act on.

The governance of cities and regions and their internationalization has thus been shaped by several concurrent forces. In the domestic arena, the emergence of globalization has overlapped with a distinct tendency across much of the world towards reduced financial and institutional support of cities and regions. In the United States, the national urban policy largely disappeared in the early 1990s (Barnes, 2005; Kaplan and James, 1990; Warren, 1990). In the UK, notions of "uneven development" and cities competing with each other have roots back to the Thatcher era but came back in vogue in the 1990s (Buck et al., 2005; see Tiebout, 1956). Similarly in Japan, the financial cutbacks during the troublesome 1990s meant that steering cities and prefectures through subsidies was no longer possible (Muramatsu, 1997).

It appears that globalization, either by itself or indirectly by the changes implemented to adapt the state to these powerful changes in its external environment, has set in motion significant changes in the relationship between central, regional, and local government. Let us now look more closely at how inter-governmental relationships have developed in our three case countries. Table 4.1 provides city managers' views on the transfer of authority among institutional levels in their respective country over the past several years.

Table 4.1 shows that the three countries have experienced three different types of changes in their inter-governmental relationships. Japan has seen a centralization of control by moving authority from the local to the central levels of government. At the same time, however, the prefectures have decentralized some of their previous control to the cities.

*Table 4.1 Transfer of authority among institutional levels in Japan, Sweden and the United States. Balance index*

| Direction of transfer of authority | Japan | Sweden | United States |
|---|---|---|---|
| From central to local government | −20.2 | −35.5 | +5.6 |
| From central to regional government | +5.9 | +4.3 | +34.1 |
| From regional to local government | +33.2 | −10.5 | +22.4 |

*Note:* The survey question was: "How would you describe the changes in the relationships between the central (federal), regional (state, prefecture), and local levels of government during the past several years?" The balance index is calculated as the percentage of respondents who indicated "agree strongly" and "agree somewhat" minus the percentage respondents indicating "disagree strongly" and "disagree somewhat". See Appendix for details.

In Sweden we see a similar increased central government control over the municipalities, although here we need to remind ourselves that this was a move from a highly decentralized arrangement. Furthermore, cities have also come under increasing control by regional institutions. Our data do not specify whether this refers to the central government administration at the country level (*länssstyrelse*) or the self-governing elected institutions at the regional level (*landsting*). In the US, finally, the most significant transfer of authority has been from the federal government to the states but there has also been a noticeable delegation of authority from the states to the cities. Thus, while Swedish cities appear to have lost some autonomy both to the regions and to central government, the US has seen authority flow in the opposite direction.

Table 4.1 also shows that there is no uniform pattern of alterations in inter-governmental relationships in the adaptation to globalization. While the three countries seek to achieve a smaller and more competitive state, institutional roles are deeply entrenched and can not be fundamentally changed in the short term. Even if the end goal may be rather similar in the three countries, the ways to get there look different depending on jurisdiction and societal expectations. The Japanese have different expectations on their local authorities than do the Americans who in turn have different expectations than the Swedes.

The centralizing pattern we see in Japan and Sweden does not resonate with the theoretical argument that domestic adaptation to globalization manifests itself inter alia in empowering subnational government while at the same time cutting back on subsidies. We therefore need to look more closely at the economics of inter-governmental relationships. Table 4.2 provides data on these issues.

When we add the economic dimension of central–local relations to the analysis a somewhat clearer picture emerges. In all three countries, but most predominantly in Japan and Sweden, unfunded (or incompletely funded) mandates have become much more common. These mandates are presumably not new programs given to cities and regions for implementation but are rather cases of incremental reductions of the financial coverage of central government programs. Japanese and Swedish responses of well above 90 percent agreeing that local government must now partially pay for the implementation of central government programs give a strong indication

*Table 4.2 Economic aspects of intergovernmental relationships (percentage respondents who strongly agree or somewhat agree with items)*

| | Japan | Sweden | United States |
|---|---|---|---|
| The city has had to take an increasing financial responsibility for delivering central government (federal) programs | 94.0 | 99.5 | 79.7 |
| The city's dependence on central (federal) and regional (state, prefecture) government for financial support has increased | 34.5 | 88.5 | 25.0 |
| N | 488 | 209 | 664 |

*Note:* See Appendix for details.

that the centralization shown in Table 4.1 is, in fact, to a very large extent an economic centralization.

This tendency towards economic centralization where central government decides on programs for which subnational government to smaller or greater extent must carry the financial burden is more consistent with the theoretical argument developed earlier in this chapter. The state seeks to boost economic competitiveness by cutting taxes and public expenditure and by relaxing its control over, as well as its support to, regions and cities. Unfunded mandates are a shrewd strategy to improve the national budget while at the same time incentivizing cities to devise new modes of service production and collaboration with societal partners. It is no coincidence that central government in Japan and Sweden have urged cities and regions to strengthen their territorial governance; indeed, regional reform in Sweden in the 1980s aimed explicitly at that objective (Nilsson, 2010).

Encouraging cities and regions to forge networks in their urban or regional space could however cause central government problems in the longer term. Inter-governmental relationships were long conceived of as a zero-sum game where empowering one institutional level usually meant that that power is taken from some other level. The governance perspective challenged that view on inter-governmental relationships (Bell and Hindmoor, 2009; Pierre and Peters, 2000). Empowering subnational government, for instance the regions, could induce regional institutions to develop networks with key strategic actors in the regional territory and thus strengthen those institutions. Such empowered regions embedded in international networks and with strong collaborative ties between regional institutions and strategic corporate and other players, are not unlikely to challenge the authority of national government on policy issues and its constitutional submission to that government more broadly.

Furthermore, globalization offers opportunities for cities and regions to escape domestic institutional control and to mobilize resources worldwide. Even in the case of the European Union, presenting yet another regulatory structure for regions and cities, there is an emphasis on inter-regional cooperation within the Union but also regions in other continents. At the same time, and by the same logic, globalization poses severe threats to cities and regions. Through the abolition of trade barriers and the deregulation of domestic markets, globalization opens up previously protected markets for overseas competition. This competition brings in labor from other countries which offer their services at significantly lower wages than domestic labor; it allows for foreign businesses to localize in the city and thus creates new or increased competition in the local market; and it urges the urban political and administrative leadership to look beyond the nation's capital for financial resources and to embark on a more entrepreneurial strategy of resource mobilization in the global landscape.

The direct and indirect linkages between subnational institutions and global forces seem to become increasingly closer. For instance, the 2008 global financial crisis has had, and will continue to have, significant ramifications for regional and local government in a large number of countries as central governments are forced to cut back on subsidies to regions and cities in order to reallocate financial resources to assist the private banking sector. Instead, government tends to emphasize "governance" as its philosophy for intergovernmental relationships. Governance here is shorthand for less top-down command and control, greater autonomy at the regional and local levels of the political system but also cutbacks in subsidies and programs to help subnational government tackle the impact of the global economy on their economy. This pattern has been particularly evident in the cases of Japan and Sweden.

## Regionalization

"Region" has become an umbrella term for a wide variety of institutional creatures between the national and the local. Some regions are quite old and have strong identities based in language or culture; we need only think of Quebec, Catalonia, or Scotland to find examples of such regions. Other regions, for instance the "economic regions" in the UK, have existed for a much shorter time period and display a much weaker regional identity. Region also refers to spaces held together by economic activities and commuting patterns. Given that the study of regions is a multidisciplinary research field, there are a number of contending approaches to, and definitions of, region.

Regionalization has clearly gained momentum during the past couple of decades. In Europe, as Newman (2000:897) shows, regionalization is driven by territorial mobilization of regional identities; changing national (political and institutional) contexts; and "the Europeanization of regional policy". These drivers of regionalization tend to reinforce each other. For instance, EU policies and programs targeting regions have incentivized central governments across Europe to adapt its regional governance structures to become eligible for such programs. A case in point is the structural funds which have driven the formation of regions or the empowerment of existing regions. The problem, as Newman (2000) points out, is that institutional reform to facilitate governance of these regions has not kept pace with the economically driven structural reform of the regions.

The empowerment of regions that come from the EU's vision of a "Europe of the Regions" (Le Galès and Lequesne, 1998) is in itself an illustration of institutional rescaling (Brenner, 1999; Goldsmith, 1993; Newman, 2000; Smyrl, 1997). While it seems clear that the continuing integration of the EU has driven the formation of organizations and networks mobilizing cities and regions in the member states, we do not know very much about the extent to which cities and regions in other regional contexts are as active in their internationalization strategies as those in Europe.

In the US, on the other hand, the concept of region seems to be much less frequently used in scholarly texts or among practitioners (see for instance Pastor et al., 2009). This might be attributed to the federal structure and the importance of the states in areas like

*Table 4.3 Consolidating the region? Cities' involvement in efforts to strengthen the region (percentages)*

| | Japan | Sweden | United States |
|---|---|---|---|
| Yes, within metropolitan region | 64.8 | 35.3 | 42.5 |
| Yes, within rural region | 21.1 | 35.3 | 12.0 |
| City declined to participate | 6.4 | 1.1 | 3.6 |
| No effort was launched | 7.6 | 28.3 | 41.9 |
| Total | 100 | 100 | 100 |
| N | 472 | 184 | 643 |

*Note:* The survey item was "Has the city been part of efforts to strengthen the (region (state, prefecture)?" The response alternatives were "Yes, within the metropolitan region which the city is part of", "Yes, within the rural region which the city is part of", "The city has chosen not to participate in such state projects", and "No such efforts have been launched". As the N number show there was a slightly higher number of internal non-responses on this item compared to other items in the survey. See Appendix for details.

economic development, a role which became more pronounced in the 1970s and 1980s (Eisner, 1989). Still, however, regions are often thought of as metropolitan areas or economically integrated areas transcending state lines (see Katz, 2000). Against this backdrop we would expect there to be noticeable differences between the three countries in terms of their attention to regional governance issues. Table 4.3 shows the variation in cities' involvement in projects aimed at strengthening the regions.

The data in Table 4.3 shows that initiatives to strengthen regional or inter-local interactions have been most common in the metropolitan regions and less so in rural areas. The metropolitan regions are both denser and more economically integrated, for example with regard to commuting patterns and public transport, and there are more substantive gains to be made from regional cooperation in such settings compared to rural areas. The data also indicate a more moderate interest among US cities in these respects compared to Japan and Sweden.

The scholarly debate accords regions a major role in economic development, the argument being that the state is becoming less inclined to target resources to growth projects but instead focuses on macroeconomic policy, while cities lack the resources and capabilities

*Table 4.4 The growing importance of regions for governance and economic development. City managers indicating that regions are becoming "much more important" or "somewhat more important" for coordination and economic development (percentages)*

| | Governance | Economic development |
|---|---|---|
| Japan | 65.5 | 77.3 |
| Sweden | 90.0 | 83.9 |
| United States | 55.6 | 63.4 |

*Note:* The survey item was: "Overall, would you say that the regional (state, prefecture) level is becoming more or less important in terms of coordination and economic development?", with one set of response alternatives for governance and one for economic development. See Appendix for details.

to manage such projects. Their role and potential as providers of governance has been given much less attention. However, along with the growing interest in regions as spaces of economic growth, issues about their governance have come to the fore. The survey asked the city managers how they assess the importance of regions in economic development and governance. Table 4.4 presents their views on these two issues.

The immediate impression from Table 4.4 is that the results substantiate the growing interest in regions in all the three countries. The lowest assessment refers to the governance role of US regions, illustrating the relatively modest interest in regions there. Swedish city managers—seemingly more convinced by the importance of regions than their Japanese and American colleagues—see the governance role of regions as more important than their role in economic development; in Japan and the United States the opposite pattern is demonstrated. Again, the argument made in parts of the globalization discourse about its tendency to produce convergence and domestic institutional change does not seem to be supported by the data. Instead, current domestic choice seems to be more reflective of the performance of the long-established institutional order. The EU-driven empowerment of regions in Europe is clearly reflected in the Swedish data but overall there is a strong distinctiveness of domestic governance arrangements in these data.

# GLOBALIZATION AND URBAN GOVERNANCE

Before we analyse inter-governmental relationships and urban governance in our three case countries we will first give a broader, comparative overview. There are two issues that are particularly pertinent to an analysis of the impact of globalization on urban governance. The first issue has to do with the changing urban agenda during globalization. The globalization argument holds that as globalization continues there will be a convergence in the agenda of local governments in different countries as part of a broader policy convergence. The path-dependent argument, on the other hand, posits that differences in perception of different challenges are still defined primarily by jurisdiction, that is, the degree to which local government is responsible for a particular sector of public service.

The second issue is related to internationalization. The rescaling theory discussed at the beginning of the chapter stipulates that globalization relaxes domestic institutional hierarchies and provides an opportunity structure for cities and regions to position themselves in international networks and markets. We need to investigate how cities and regions in our case countries implement internationalization strategies and how such efforts are coordinated among local authorities within the countries.

## The Changing Urban Political Agenda

How do local governments in Japan, Sweden, and the United States assess different types of challenges? Table 4.5 gives an overview of how city managers identify various challenges to their cities.

Some responses do not strike the reader as very unexpected. The demographic development in Japan and to a lesser extent in Sweden and the challenge it entails is well-known. Similarly, about 50 percent of the city managers in the three countries see citizens' expectation on public service as a major problem; again, given the financial constraints and cutbacks this pattern should only be expected. And, given the low levels of immigration into Japan, it is no surprise that ethnic diversity and immigration does not pose a major problem in Japan. Other responses are more confounding. Less than 5 percent of Swedish city managers see local environmental issues as a very big problem. The low score is explained by the fact that the local

*Table 4.5 Challenges to local governments in Japan, Sweden and the United States. Percentage of city managers who identify various challenges as a "major problem" (percentages)*

| | Japan | Sweden | United States |
|---|---|---|---|
| Protecting the local environment | 47.9 | 4.5 | 33.3 |
| A weaker local tax base | 84.0 | 47.1 | 26.7 |
| Citizens' service expectations | 49.7 | 49.5 | 51.2 |
| Increasing unemployment | 27.5 | 44.8 | 8.4 |
| Increasing number of elderly people | 80.7 | 53.8 | 20.5 |
| Declining local industries | 55.1 | 17.6 | 18.1 |
| Ethnic diversity, immigration | 4.3 | 6.2 | 20.0 |
| Weak political leadership | 6.0 | 21.1 | 14.0 |
| Inefficiencies in service production | 32.9 | 7.2 | 9.0 |
| Increasing wages for city employees | 31.5 | 11.9 | 28.5 |
| Size of local authority is too small | 10.9 | 27.9 | 6.8 |
| N | 487 | 206 | 664 |

*Note:* The survey item was "Which are the main challenges and problems confronting the city today?" The response alternatives were "major problem", "minor problem", "not a problem" and "irrelevant". See Appendix for details.

environmental protection administration operates almost as a local subsidiary to the state, tightly regulated by legislation. Although environmental protection represents a significant organizational commitment to the local authorities they have only very limited autonomy on the issue.[3]

The (population) size of the municipality is an intriguing issue. In Japan the average size in 2013 is around 74,000, compared with about 32,000 for Swedish municipalities and around 17,500 for the US.[4] Japan recently completed a major amalgamation reform in its local government system, reducing the number of municipalities to less than half of what it was a decade ago (see below). In Sweden, a similar amalgamation reform was implemented several decades ago, ending in the early 1970s with 284 municipalities (current figure is 290). In Japan, some 11 percent of the city managers insist that their municipality is too small and similarly in Sweden about 28 percent indicate that the small size of the municipality is a major problem. The corresponding US figure is less than 7 percent; a number to be interpreted with caution as the sample of US municipalities excluded the smallest and biggest municipalities.[5]

The explanation for this pattern, as well as the cross-national variation in Table 4.5 more broadly, is jurisdiction and the relationship between tasks and resources. Cities define issues as major problems when they have a responsibility for service and programs. The size of the municipality only becomes a problem if the local authority has jurisdiction, and responsibility, in a wide range of policy areas. As long as the size of the municipality, and thereby it's financial and organizational capabilities, corresponds to its governance and service responsibilities, the local authority can avoid being overloaded. Thus, Japanese city managers see the demographic situation as a major problem because care of the elderly falls under local government's jurisdiction.

If mergers between local authorities do not suffice to create economies of scale (or if there is strong opposition towards mergers), various forms of collaboration among local governments have become an attractive alternative in many countries. We have seen increasing cooperation among local authorities in Japan (Jacobs, 2004), Sweden (Lundqvist, 1998) and the United States (Feiock, 2004).

The pattern in Table 4.5 rejects the globalization hypothesis. Cities continue to define problems and the urban policy agenda according to their responsibilities, and there have not been any major changes in local governments' formal responsibilities that can be directly related to globalization, although keeping in mind the increasing unfunded mandates and the greater self-reliance now expected of cities and regions. If there is convergence it should be attributed to factors other than global pressures, primarily a growing commonality in the problems cities are confronted with or citizens' expectation on public service. For instance, Japanese and Swedish cities have care of the elderly in their respective responsibility hence the increasing similarity between two countries in that respect.

## Internationalization

The other aspect of inter-governmental relationships that we will study in more detail is internationalization. How do cities view the significance of international partnerships and how are internationalization strategies implemented? While nation–state governments, at least initially, tend to surround overseas ventures of this type with some degree of diplomatic pomp and banner waving, cities and regions tend to be less programmatic about their internationalization projects. Instead, they usually go about such enterprises with characteristic, pragmatic focus on results. It is indicative that subnational internationalization tends to suffer from some degree of democratic deficit (van der Heiden, 2010); cities and regions tend to see internationalization as part of the agenda for the political executive, and not a topic of political debate. Internationalization projects can be costly and the returns are uncertain and long-term, making them difficult to defend in public debate on how to allocate the city's resources (Beauregard and Pierre, 2000).

Table 4.6 gives a comparative overview of how city managers perceive the importance of developing overseas partnerships. The table seems to tell the different stories about the processes of cities' international efforts.

Among the three case countries, Japan's cities seem to have the longest experience of building international partnerships. To them, these projects have not become more important recently; almost 40 percent indicate that they always were important. However, the same percentage responded that international partnerships have never been important. In Sweden, and even more so in the United States, these international strategies appear to be more recent.

*Table 4.6 Local governments' strategies to build partnerships with local governments in other countries (percentages)*

| | Japan | Sweden | United States |
|---|---|---|---|
| Has become more important | 8.4 | 53.1 | 39.0 |
| Has become less important | 5.1 | 2.4 | 1.7 |
| Was always important | 38.2 | 6.7 | 13.1 |
| Was never important | 8.6 | 31.6 | 25.6 |
| Irrelevant | 39.6 | 6.2 | 20.7 |
| Sum | 99.9 | 100 | 100 |
| N | 488 | 206 | 664 |
| Balance | +32.9 | +25.8 | +24.8 |

*Note:* The balance is calculated as the sum of "has become more important" and "was always important" minus the sum of "has become less important" and "was never important".

It is striking that internationalization is not something which all cities engage in. We mentioned previously that rescaling does not present cities with an imperative but with a choice, an opportunity structure. The pattern in Table 4.6, not least the Japanese responses where roughly the same number of cities indicate that international partnerships always were important and that such partnerships are "irrelevant", seems to lend support to that statement.

An additional explanation for this pattern could simply be that the three countries are not on the same timeline with regard to internationalization. Japanese cities were encouraged by central government to set up cross-border partnerships in the late 1980s, hence the response from many cities that such partnerships have always been important. For Sweden, internationalization increased and was more strategically designed as a result of the EU membership in the mid-1990s. It is possible that American cities close to the Canadian and Mexican borders may have become more inclined to develop cross-border partnerships after NAFTA and its extension came into effect. These issues require more investigation. However, Jesuit and Sych (2012) show that local economic development levels and proximity to national borders may have an effect on cities' inclination to form networks with cities in other countries, for instance cities in Michigan who forge partnerships with Canadian cities.

In addition, as we pointed out earlier the international exposure in relative terms of the US economy is smaller than that of the Swedish or Japanese economies. It is reasonable to expect that cities with a local economy to some degree operating in international markets will be more inclined to pursue internationalization projects compared to cities where there is little or no international exposure.

We will now add more context to the analysis by looking in somewhat more detail on internationalization strategies and governance reform in the three countries. We will focus on two aspects related to inter-governmental relationships; internationalization and governance reform. With regard to internationalization, we will not make any attempt at going into depth on individual internationalization projects. Instead we will focus on how cities use collective action and international networks and organizations to pursue their objectives overseas. As regards governance reform, the focus is on changes in the local or regional government system and broad changes in governance. Consistent with the overarching theme of the book we are interested to what degree changes can be linked to international pressures and norms.

## JAPAN

### Internationalization

The hollowing out (*kudoka*) of the Japanese industry following the Plaza Accord in 1985 and the appreciation of the yen in 1993 (*endaka*) drove cities and prefectures to develop international networks and frequently also to set up offices overseas. As mentioned already, these strategies were strongly encouraged by the central government. Cities pursued bilateral contacts but also regionally coordinated efforts of building cross-border networks, not least with mainland China. A case in point is the local authorities on the southern island of Kyushu where Kita-Kyushu, Fukuoka, and Shimonoseki teamed up to cooperate with Pusan (Korea) and Dalian (China) around the Yellow Sea and have also formed an association.

Japan has developed a large number of organizations to promote international trade and internationalization more broadly. A key actor in the internationalization of local governments is the Council of Local Authorities for International Relations (CLAIR). CLAIR was established in 1988 as a cooperative body. Local authorities are dues-paying members and fund the organization directly. However, CLAIR was not set up by the local authorities themselves but by the Ministry of Internal Affairs and Communication (MIC) who encouraged cities to set up the organization.

Thus, the organization has a dual nature; it reflects MIC's ideas about how to internationalize local government at the same time as it is built as a cooperative body for local authorities and prefectural governments. Thus, the organizational model builds on the active involvement—and financial commitment—of the cities at the same time as it gives government a channel to guide the cities and to monitor their internationalization efforts. This duality is further substantiated by *amakudari* appointments or recruitments from the Governors' Association and the City Association to its senior leadership.[6] In addition, most of the staff is on secondment from cities or prefectures. It is clear that an important role of CLAIR is to serve as a network bringing together government institutions, subnational government, and their related associations in the sector of internationalization. It is an organization of, and for, local governments operating "under the shadow of hierarchical authority" (see Scharpf, 1994:41).

Given the decline in the economy, it has become increasingly difficult for local authorities to prioritize internationalization projects when weighed against other public service areas:

> Local authorities are today in a difficult financial situation. The peak of internationalization was when Japan was going well and local governments were awash with tax revenues. Now, growth is low and resources are limited. There is also the problem of an ageing population and the need to invest in welfare services. This means that it has become more difficult to justify spending on internationalization. More and more people are calling for internationalization efforts that have concrete and immediate effect.[7]

It is clear that the financial crisis and the ensuing cutbacks in local and prefectural government have drawn attention to the dues paid to CLAIR. A substantive part of the organization's budget goes into sustaining offices in major financial and trading cities overseas; New York, London, Paris, Singapore, Seoul, Beijing, and Sydney. The problem with keeping these offices in not unattractive stations is that CLAIR members have problems matching benefits with the significant costs. Thus, in 2009 the Osaka prefecture announced that it no longer wants to pay the dues to CLAIR because of dissatisfaction with the activities and efficiency of the organization.[8] Previously, many of the bigger Japanese cities had their own offices in key economic cities around the world, which made it challenging for them to pay the membership dues to CLAIR. As a result of the financial setback, many of these cities have closed their offices and now use CLAIR's offices.

Japanese cities relied earlier on sister city bilateral contacts but are now reassessing their strategies: "The sister city institution has developed from being mainly about cultural exchange towards being based more on strategic considerations. The prospect of economic exchange is becoming more and more important. CLAIR has to prioritize economic exchange because they get money from the local authorities and they ask increasingly often questions related to economic exchange."[9]

CLAIR is the key structure for the collective internationalization of cities and prefectures in Japan. Its purpose is not to match individual Japanese cities with suitable partners overseas. Instead it defines its role as a provider of information to local and regional government. In addition, it is an important interface between different tiers of government in the context of internationalization.

## Governance Reform

Any assessment of inter-governmental relationships and governance reform in Japanese local government must depart from two important aspects of the Japanese institutional system; the historically strong centralization of the system and the significance of inter-regional relationships (see Muramatsu, 1997). Both aspects speak directly to the overarching question of to what extent and how globalization has impacted inter-governmental relationships.

The classical model of Japanese inter-governmental relationships has been that of a centralized and hierarchical model with some degree of institutional friction and disagreement between center and periphery (Muramatsu, 1997). The Japanese state has drawn on a wide variety of policy instruments such as tax incentives and rules to ensure subnational compliance. The financial crisis and subsequent cutbacks in public funds have meant that tax incentives and subsidies are no longer feasible policy instruments. Inter-governmental relationships are therefore, as we will see, becoming somewhat more negotiated and there is a growing emphasis on "governance", both in the vertical relationship and also horizontally at the urban and regional levels of the political system.

The strong centralization, or what Kamo (2000:2147) calls the "unipolar urban hierarchy" of Japanese society, has historical roots although globalization further reinforced Tokyo's dominant position in the urban landscape. Several Japanese industrial centers were deeply embedded in international markets during the "economic miracle" of the early post-war decades. In the 1980s, however, global exchanges began to swing the other way. Globalization hit Tokyo which had the benefits of being the political and corporate center of the nation and thus in a better position to handle the globalization pressure than most other Japanese cities. Tokyo was the key international point of contact which helped elevate the city to a "world city". Thus, globalization and unipolarization took place side by side, one reinforcing the other.

The problem of Tokyo's centrality in Japan was not new. In the

1920s, the government encouraged the concentration of corporate headquarters to Tokyo. Before 1920, Tokyo and Osaka were equally significant cities, with Tokyo as the political center and Osaka as the manufacturing and commercial center. After the Second World War, several corporate headquarters relocated from Osaka to Tokyo, thus starting the decline of Osaka.

The accumulation of political and corporate control functions is a self-reinforcing process and what became known as the "Tokyo problem" is shorthand for an over-concentration of people and economic functions. These problems were felt both within Tokyo itself but also across the country, not least in Osaka which saw a continuing loss of companies, corporate headquarters, and skilled labor to the nation's capital (Hill and Fujita, 1995). Inter-regional differences, even the birth rate, continued to increase, eventually leading to high land value and high costs of living in Tokyo.

In the 1980s and early 1990s, a government Commission assessed the need for administrative reform (1987–1992; see Chapter 5). The Commission concluded that Tokyo's key problem was the concentration of political and administrative functions which drove land value and costs of living. Initiatives were launched to alleviate the pressures on Tokyo and to shift some administrative and economic functions from Tokyo to Osaka, for instance ventures in the high risk-high yield future markets. There were also initiatives from within the Kansai region where Osaka is located, most importantly the Kansai international airport and the Science Park.

In 1999, a so-called "package (or omnibus) law" for decentralization was implemented in order to address the growing inter-regional differences in Japan. However, many politicians and bureaucrats opposed decentralization. The concentration of political, administrative, financial, and corporate leadership functions was deemed necessary to sustain Tokyo's position as a global city; indeed, had the "package law" been altogether successful, the unintended result could have been the erosion of Tokyo's international standing (Kamo, 2000).

Globalization has impacted Japanese subnational government and inter-governmental relationships in different ways. In the 1980s, globalization was mainly impacting Tokyo as the international gateway to Japan. This was a time when much of the rest of the country could enjoy increasing export revenues from their industry. From the late 1980s when Japan had to appreciate its currency several times, and even more so during the troubled 1990s, globalization hit the Japanese economy across the board. Tokyo is not an industrial city and was spared from the immediate ramifications of industrial decline and "hollowing out" but took a major hit in 1997 when the financial centers crumbled and several of the big commercial banks filed for bankruptcy.

The regional and local levels of the Japanese political system have undergone significant structural changes during the past couple of years. There has been a process of local government merger, reducing the number of municipalities from 3000 to about 1500. The key driver of this process has been an inability of smaller municipalities to shoulder increasing service challenges, for instance the growing percentage of elderly people. Thus, the past several decades have seen a growing call for municipal mergers in several regions to maintain and improve the quality of municipal public services and also to increase the efficiency in municipal administration and service production. The Law for "Exceptional Measures on Municipal Mergers" (originally enacted as early as 1965) allows for "exceptional measures" to facilitate the voluntary merger of municipalities. The Law which was extended in 1975, 1985 and 1995 enables municipal mergers on a voluntary base. This model of regulation has proven successful; the number of municipalities has decreased from 3232 (1999) to 2326 (2005) and 1822 (2006). There has also been a strong interest in inter-local partnerships both as a complement and an alternative to merger (Jacobs, 2004).

The regional level of government has also been subject to reform. The recession in the Japanese economy during the first 5–6 years of the 1990s and the deep financial crisis in 1997 meant that the government announced new roles for cities and prefectures. Prefectures in particular should adopt a softer, less hierarchical governance role and forge strategic alliances with key players in their territory. Given the tough financial situation, prefectures could no longer rely on subsidies to steer businesses and other key players in the region. In 1999, a senior official in the Osaka prefecture described in an interview this emerging governance role:

> The role of the prefectural government will shift towards a coordinating role; coordinating local governments, public corporations and private actors. The prefecture will now have to rely on 'encouragement' but without money. The prefectural government can no longer use the

> SME funds as incentives to private businesses to change their behavior. However, companies will listen to what we are saying.[10]

There is also discussion about changing the regional institutional organization by replacing the current 47 prefectures with about 20 bigger administrative units with more autonomy than the prefectures. This is the essence of the *doshu-sei* reform. It is advocated by much of the business community and also by the LDP in the latest elections.

## SWEDEN

### Internationalization

In 2009, about a third of the local authorities in Sweden were involved in a cross-border partnership.[11] After Sweden joined the EU in the mid-1990s, cities and regions set up and implemented extensive internationalization strategies.

Swedish local authorities pursue international contacts individually, in groups defined by regions, and through SALAR, the national association for local and regional government. International strategies are predominantly aimed at the EU and its institutions. The regionally coordinated internationalization has been driven by the EU's regional structural funds partnerships. These partnerships have probably been important in fostering cooperation among the local authorities. Cooperative behavior is also clearly visible among regions in northern Sweden, within the so-called "Europaforum Norra Sverige" [Europe Forum North Sweden] where four counties [*län*] coordinate their interactions with the EU. The Council of European Municipalities and Regions (CEMR), a lobby organization for subnational government in Brussels is also an important component of municipalities' and regions' internationalization.

SALAR's main contacts with the municipalities and regions in the context of internationalization are the so-called EU coordinators. Internationalization is driven both by a pursuit of local and regional interests vis-à-vis the EU and developing networks to increase knowledge in the local or regional organization.

The role of SALAR is somewhat complicated since not all local authorities and regions share the same objective in their internationalization strategies. Some may lobby to secure infrastructural investment to their city or region, something which pits regions or cities in competition and places SALAR in a difficult situation. "We cannot represent all local authorities and regions since different regions make different priorities".[12] SALAR has a strong focus on the benefits that internationalization offers its members. Regions are primarily oriented towards the EU while local authorities tend to have a broader internationalization strategy. SALAR frequently organizes conferences and workshops where local and regional authorities can learn from each other and exchange ideas and experiences. Internationalization is thus a high priority for SALAR; "the objective is that the EU and its institutional perspective will be mainstreamed in every local authority. Pursuing international contacts or mobilizing resources from the EU should be a natural component of the administration".[13]

Internationalization is to some degree about representing territorially based institutions in international arenas. At the same time, however, different sectors in the local or regional administration have more specific needs for international contacts such as exploring ideas for improving services or cutting costs. SALAR sees a potential problem with the strategy of internationalizing sectors instead of territorially defined institutions as bigger local authorities may benefit more from that strategy than smaller authorities.[14]

Local authorities frequently engage in the so-called local partnership program (*kommunalt partnerskapsprogram, KP*). The typical pattern is that individual local authorities, using SIDA funds, create aid projects in developing countries where the basic idea is to transfer knowledge in areas such as environmental protection technology, water and sewage systems, waste disposal, education, that is, areas where the local authority has extensive knowledge.[15] SALAR also pursues aid projects through the company SALA IDA, created in 2000.[16]

SALAR has on several occasions evaluated its role in the internationalization of regions and cities. Member surveys were conducted in 2008 and 2010. The 2008 survey indicated some criticism among the members against the ways in which SALAR defined its role in internationalization. The 2010 survey suggested that members were now somewhat more pleased with SALAR. However, the 2010 survey also showed that there is some misfit between the priorities and capabilities of SALAR on the one hand and members' priorities and expectations on the other. For instance, some local authorities want SALAR to support them in terms of developing projects and financial matters; "the local authorities want a type of support which SALAR cannot give". Similarly, local authorities expect SALAR to monitor EU activities in the field of rural area support, "an issue which is quite marginal in SALAR". On the other hand, policies and regulations on public sector support in public service provision which potentially affect competition in markets, an issue which is extremely important to SALAR, received only scant attention from the organization's members.[17]

SALAR's role as a promoter of internationalization of local and regional government has become increasingly accentuated over the past 10–15 years. Unlike CLAIR in Japan which is devoted solely to the purpose of internationalization, SALAR performs this task as part of its more general role as a national association for local and regional government. That means that members are not likely to assess the relationship between its internationalization benefits in relation to their membership dues to SALAR. Furthermore, while CLAIR seems to be mainly demand-driven, SALAR has been more proactive, particularly in the early years of the EU membership when local governments and regions had very limited knowledge on how to engage the institutions and networks in Brussels.

## Governance Reform

In the 1950s, Sweden was divided into some 2500 municipalities. 25 years later that figure had decreased by close to 90 percent to 274 municipalities.[18] The expanding welfare state required local authorities with strong organizational and financial capabilities to deliver a wide range of welfare programs. Contrary to widespread concerns, the massive merger did not have any detrimental ramifications on local democracy, in fact the opposite. Citizens' knowledge on local political issues increased; the media provided better coverage of local politics in the new, bigger municipalities; the political parties were invigorated and presented voters with more distinct choices; and public service improved (Strömberg and Westerståhl, 1983).

The new, bigger local authorities also became much more active in economic development (Pierre, 1992). The late 1970s and 1980s were difficult years for Swedish industry with structural changes in shipbuilding, textile, and steel. Swedish labor costs were not competitive in the global markets where Japanese and Korean producers could deliver at much lower costs. The 1970s and the early 1980s saw government playing a major role in accommodating labor and supporting cities and regions hit by overseas competition. Soon, however, industrial policy took a more future-oriented aim. Support to declining industries was gradually reduced while future-oriented sectors of the economy gained increasing policy attention (Henning, 1987; Pierre, 1992). From the early 1990s onwards it became increasingly clear that cities and regions should not expect government to bail out declining industries or support urban and regional regeneration.

This trajectory of economic restructuring in the face of global competition and the gradual decline in government support to distressed businesses and regions propelled a further local and regional commitment to economic development issues. At both the local and regional levels of government, the first several years saw economic development as a top political priority in many cities and regions. Gradually, however cities and regions created autonomous organizations to deal with economic development, thus removing the issue from the daily agenda and allowing professionals rather than politicians to work with economic development projects.

The late 1990s was also a time of regional institutional reform (Nilsson, 2010). Following decades of studies and investigations, new regions were formed in different parts of the country and given more autonomy and a wider agenda. A key objective of reform was to facilitate stronger regional governance. Also, given the EU membership adapting regional institutions to the requirements of the structural funds and other forms of support was essential.

In sum, governance reform has been characterized first by extensive municipal merger and the growth of the welfare state, then by economic restructuring and later by the EU membership and a growing responsibility for economic development. Urban politics is sometimes said to be torn between promoting democracy and governance on the one hand and efficiency on the other (Keating, 1991) and much of the reform in Sweden displays this goal conflict. During the past decade much progress has been made in improving the efficiency and effectiveness in service delivery through public management reform and innovation. Apart from some degree of organizational changes, however, the overall pattern of local governance is one of stability. At the regional level new institutional systems were launched in selected regions in the 1990s and early 2000s and there has since then been an extended process of institutionalization and consolidation (Nilsson, 2010).

## THE UNITED STATES

### Internationalization

We saw previously (Table 4.6) that US local governments are somewhat less inclined to embark on internationalization ventures compared to Japanese or Swedish local governments. American cities and regions do not have the same incentives as their European counterparts to look beyond national borders. While cities and counties on those borders tend to be more active in pursuing international ventures, the overwhelming majority of US municipalities have very little international exposure. That said, 39 percent of American city managers indicate that internationalization has become more important.

The main manifestation of collective action in international arenas for US municipalities is the International City/County Management Association (ICMA).[19] A membership-based organization (there are also 50 corporate members), ICMA has been internationally oriented since it was created in 1914. Individual members are predominantly American but also from a number of other countries. During the last 20 years the organization has expanded its activities in the developing world where network building and consulting for donor organizations have become major organizational tasks.

ICMA has developed the so-called "City Links" fellowship program to foster international contacts among cities. ICMA assesses the needs and demands in the context of capacity building in a city in the developing world and finds a suitable matching US city to help develop that capacity. So far more than 50 such "city links" have been created. The initiative to create a link comes from donor organizations or ICMA.

ICMA works with 25 affiliate organizations, including and beyond the Commonwealth group of countries. Its main roles are related to the information and dissemination aspects of development. The Knowledge Network is organized as an online-based shared resource, managed by ICMA in partnership with the "Alliance for Innovation" and The School of Public Affairs at Arizona State

University. The Knowledge Network is one of ICMA's biggest projects, containing more than 25,000 pieces of content from development work, case studies, and so on, from members and other sources. There is now some effort to get the 50 corporate members more involved in the Knowledge Network.

"The Knowledge Network has clearly made ICMA more competitive in development", says a senior ICMA official.[20] ICMA has developed its agenda to include project funding, for example in China and Lebanon; it supports e-learning projects funded by the World Bank initiative; it has developed a certificate program in financial management and has sold it to several Asian countries. There is a market for donor organizations' aid where organizations like ICMA offer consultancies for donor organizations like the World Bank.

"A bit of tension" has been noted in the last few years between ICMA's domestic and international member orientation, mainly due to the economic downturn. The international side of the organization is rapidly expanding in developing countries and countries in conflict. "Local government is recognized as a force in economic development and in the promotion of competitiveness and stability. The World Bank is pushing the competitiveness issue".[21]

Thus, ICMA's international activities are guided less by the strategic interests of US cities but more by the needs in developing countries and international donor organizations' programs. As we have seen in Japan and to some extent also in Sweden, uncertainty of the role and goals of the collective action coupled with the economic crisis easily triggers critique against the efficiency of collective action in the area of internationalization. In the case of ICMA that criticism seems to be directed at the focus on cities in developing countries instead of domestic issues. Since ICMA does not define its role as a broker of strategic contacts between US and overseas cities it is likely that American cities and regions pursue internationalization outside collective arrangements (see Fry et al., 1989; Fry, 1998, 2013; Hobbs, 1994).

## Governance Reform

Inter-governmental relationships take on a slightly different meaning in the federal system than in unitary states. Given that the federal system emphasizes states which are hierarchically placed between the federal and local levels, reform becomes more complicated to implement compared to unitary systems where reform can be more distinctly top-down. Inter-governmental reform in the United States is thus described by an observer:

> Reform is episodic; it gets attention on a 15 years basis. One concept has been that states should focus on infrastructure and schools, the federal level should be responsible for healthcare, and local government should mainly do place-based services. Changes post-9/11 have placed an enormous burden on local government. There is now a huge stress in the system. The system is very difficult to change. The easiest solution is to set up new bodies outside the existing system to deliver new tasks.[22]

If there thus is some uncertainty about how to best design inter-governmental relationships, scholarly assessments of change in the American local governments convey an image of stability. Summarizing an analysis of local government reform in the United States, Dollery et al. (2008:14; see Svara and Hoene, 2008) state that "formal and informal changes have been incremental and continuous and the result of adjusting to other developments rather than the product of explicit redesign of local government as a system". This observation raises the issue of what these other developments might be, particularly if international influences have been a driver of reform. There is very little to suggest that that has been the case. A well-placed observer in Washington, DC with experience from consultancy and public service puts the matter rather bluntly, "there have been no international influences on inter-governmental relationships in the United States. We have our own mess."[23]

Unlike the two other case countries, the United States has not experienced municipal mergers designed and implemented top-down; there have been cases of annexations but not a policy of merger. This pattern may perhaps be explained by the federal system and the (relatively speaking) more limited role of local government in service provision compared to local governments in welfare-state countries.

If thus the local government system and local governance is characterized by considerable stability, there is a great deal of innovation and change in public management. As we will discuss in the next chapter, the United States was at the forefront of public management reform during the 1990s and 2000s. Much of this innovation took place at the state and local levels (see, for instance, Brudney et al., 1999; Moore, 1995). In terms of governance reform, perhaps the most salient issue is related to the virtues of the council-manager and the council-mayor model of local government. Again, however, there is very little evidence of any international influences on this debate.[24]

## CONCLUDING DISCUSSION

The impact of globalization on inter-governmental relationships and on urban and regional governance has primarily been indirect and has emerged through different channels. One source of global pressures on cities and regions has been the intensified structural change in the economy that has followed in the wake of the deregulated international markets and the removal of trade barriers. In addition, national institutions in many countries would previously have mitigated those pressures by compensating affected cities and regions for the economic damage of international competition. However, globalization underscored the need for government to keep a strict economy and to promote urban competitiveness rather than sustaining industries that were no longer competitive. The combined effect of intensified economic restructuring and the decreasing role of the state as a dampening factor meant that cities and regions were more exposed to a more aggressive competition than previously.

In terms of inter-governmental relationships, the policy shift in central government towards subnational self-reliance was normally associated with some degree of decentralization but also a growing tendency toward unfunded, or insufficiently funded, mandates for local governments. In terms of rescaling, then, it would appear as if the gradual dismantling of national government's protecting subnational government from the impact of globalization and the reduced financial support to cities and regions have created strong incentives for these subnational systems to embark on internationalization projects.

Are the changes we see path-dependent or has globalization meant a distinct change of course of reform? In Japan and Sweden in particular, it is clear that inter-governmental relationships have been redefined since the late 1980s or early 1990s. Whether the main driver of this definition is globalization in itself, or outcomes of domestic strategies of adaptation to globalization, or the ascendance of neo-liberal regimes in many countries during this time period is a very complex issue; the most intuitive answer would be that it is a combination of all of these factors.

It is clear, however, that there has been a rescaling of political authority in these two countries, and that the process has been driven by central government. By increasing unfunded mandates, reducing subsidies, and emphasizing governance rather than top-down command and control, government has provided cities and regions with strong impetus for internationalization. The EU membership, itself a powerful driver of rescaling (Brenner, 1999), provided additional incentives for Swedish regions and cities to approach Union institutions without consulting central government.

Japanese cities and prefectures were equally encouraged by their government to forge international contacts in the wake of trade agreements and currency appreciations in the 1980s and 1990s. The change in policy was less discrete and more subtle in terms of where the international partners were located than was the case with the Swedish EU membership but it still represented a new course of policy.

While it thus is safe to say that globalization, directly or indirectly, has entailed a formative moment in inter-governmental relationships in Japan and Sweden, the picture is less clear with regard to the case of the United States. Internationalization is less widespread among US cities than is the case in Japan and Sweden although there appears to be attention to overseas strategic networks. Regions and regionalization is also less salient in the United States, compared to the two other case countries. The evidence therefore would support the hypothesis that reform is path-dependent and that globalization has not significantly altered the course or objectives of reform.

## NOTES

1. See the Appendix for details.
2. Officer, Board Secretariat, SALAR, May 4, 2009.
3. My thanks to Lennart J. Lundqvist for explaining the intricacies of local environmental policy and administration.
4. The US figure is based on municipalities. If we include townships, the average population size is about 8700. There are differences among the states in the structure of local government and in the meanings of terms such as "township". Also, local government units in the US may overlap, so that individuals may live in counties, municipalities, and townships simultaneously. The use of the

statistics on municipalities represents the closest approximation of the term in the other two countries.

5. The sample design is described in the Appendix.
6. *Amakudari* (in translation "descent from heaven") refers to the recruitment of former senior government officials to senior posts in private businesses or other organizations, usually outside the realm of government (see Colignon, 2003). Recently, *amakudari* has been criticised for contributing to corruption and after the 2009 election proposals were put forward to outlaw the procedure. The present *amakudari* arrangement provides government with an informal channel to steer and monitor CLAIR's activities.
7. Senior official, Exchange and Information Department, Council of Local Authorities for International Relations (CLAIR), October 7, 2009.
8. There was later an arrangement between CLAIR and the Osaka prefecture to reduce the membership fee in return for the prefecture's remaining a member of the organization.
9. Interview with two senior officials, Exchange and Information Department, CLAIR, October 7, 2009.
10. SME funds refer to moneys devoted to develop the small and medium-sized industry. Senior Researcher, Osaka Prefectural Institute for Advanced Industrial Development, November 15, 1999.
11. Officer, Board Secretariat, SALAR, May 4, 2009.
12. Official, International Section, SALAR, May 24, 2010.
13. Official, International Section, SALAR, May 24, 2010.
14. Interestingly, the SALAR staff are aware of their Japanese colleague CLAIR's problems with securing support from their members. The internationalization of Swedish local authorities is not related to the economic cycle: "even in recession we are members of the EU". Official, International Section, Swedish Association of Local Authorities and Regions, May 24, 2010.
15. SIDA is the Swedish International Development Agency.
16. Officer, Board Secretariat, SALAR, May 4, 2009.
17. Officer, Board Secretariat, SALAR, May 4, 2009.
18. The current number of municipalities is 290.
19. In addition, there is also Sister Cities International (SCI) which coordinates and develops cities bilateral international contacts.
20. Senior official, ICMA, April 19, 2010.
21. Senior official, ICMA, April 19, 2010.
22. Executive Director for major consultancy, September 3, 2008.
23. Executive Director for major consultancy, September 3, 2008.
24. In the UK there has been a related debate about the elected mayor model (see Pierre, 2011b, and the relevant literature cited therein).

# 5. Modernizing the state: administrative reform

The true test of a good government is its aptitude and tendency to produce a good administration.
Publius, *Federalist* No. 68 (Hamilton et al., 1961:414)

The New Public Management has obfuscated any discussion of political power and left us with only a managerial leitmotif that has made the notion of "political" almost problematic.
(Ventriss, 2000:505)

In 1979, following a convincing electoral triumph for the Conservative Party, Margaret Thatcher was appointed Prime Minister of the UK. Elected in 1980 and sworn into office in January 1981, Ronald Reagan became President of the United States. While there were differences between the two leaders in terms of specific policies, Mrs. Thatcher and Ronald Reagan shared a conviction that one of the priorities of their respective governments should be a profound modernization of the state. Both believed that the state had taken precedence over the market and that a fundamental shift was required from the growth of the public sector and Keynesian economics to "unleashing" the market and to embark on a monetaristic economic policy (Pierson, 1994). This crusade against the "privileged" civil service (Hood, 1995; Savoie, 1994) and the public sector more broadly would have a deep and lasting influence on the state, not only in the homelands of Mrs. Thatcher and Ronald Reagan but across the world.

In both countries, the modernization project evolved into an ideologically driven all-out attack on public services, the public sector, and public sector employees. This "new politics of administrative reform", as it could be called, soon spread to Canada, Australia, and New Zealand (Savoie, 1994). The second generation of state modernization in the Thatcher–Reagan neo-liberal philosophy was implemented largely as a result of pressures from transnational institutions such as the IMF and the World Bank, targeting countries in central and Southeast Asia (Turner, 2002), Europe, Africa (Manning, 2001; Schick, 1998), and to some extent Latin America. Thus, in a short period of time, a large number of countries at different levels of development, with different administrative traditions, different institutional arrangements, and different public sector size and scope, all found themselves implementing or contemplating New Public Management (henceforth NPM) reform (Christensen and Laegreid, 2011; Pollitt and Bouckaert, 2011).[1]

Was this global wave of similar administrative reform a manifestation of globalization? Or, can the similarity in reform in different jurisdictions simply be explained by a similarity in the problems and challenges facing those governments in terms of increasing costs for delivering public services? Does the NPM campaign of administrative reform represent an imposition of Washington Consensus-led neoliberal ideas on countries regardless of their own preferences, or was the global common denominator a growing critique among citizens and clients against high taxes and poor services? To what extent was administrative reform path-dependent to the various countries and to what degree did it represent a breach with administrative tradition?

This chapter will first discuss the drivers of administrative reform and the role of international organizations in the promotion of such reform. We then turn to the in-depth analysis of administrative reform in the three case countries.

## DRIVERS OF ADMINISTRATIVE REFORM

Administrative reform is essentially about modernizing the structure and modus operandi of the state. The concept of administrative reform is not very easy to boil down to a narrow range of issues. It tends to be used as an umbrella concept for such diverse issues as public organization change, public management, deregulation, transparency, public service production, responsiveness and accountability, citizen engagement, and public markets (see Pollitt and Bouckaert, 2011).

A key issue in understanding the relationship between globalization and state modernization has to do with the principal drivers of administrative reform. One type of reform driver is derived from changes in the relationship between the public sector and its external environment. According to Perry et al. (1996), the growing disjuncture between constitutional provisions and functional demands for administration has been a powerful incentive for administrative reform. National civil service systems have been expected to engage in new roles, or perform its roles differently, hence the pressure to change the structure and function of the civil service and the public sector more broadly (Peters and Pierre, 2007). The assumption that such a "disjuncture" between organizational norms and external expectations represents a pressure for reform is central to institutional theory (see Brunsson, 1989; Brunsson and Olsen, 1993).

Second, administrative reform can also be propelled by "epistemic communities" (Haas, 1992) promoting "ideas in good currency" (Schön, 1983). There is a high degree of similarity in the types of challenges that the public sector in developed countries has been confronting in the last 10–15 years: increasing costs in public service delivery, a demographic "time bomb", growing dissatisfaction among recipients of public service for lack of flexibility and proper service, and inefficiencies caused by (real or perceived) poor management of public organizations (Peters, 2001). There was a universal search for administrative reform ideas that would help governments address those problems and a tendency for governments to emulate each other's solution to those problems.

Third, globalization can be a powerful driver of administrative reform insofar as it places an imperative on states to reform the public sector in specific ways with specific objectives. However, the relationship between global pressures and the specific measures that government chooses to implement in administrative reform is more complex than the rather straightforward globalization thesis suggests (compare Lynn, 2001). As this chapter will show, there are other forces at play which may yield similar patterns of reform in different countries. Global pressures certainly play a role but sometimes in more subtle ways than is often argued. As Christopher Pollitt (2001:936, italics in original) suggests, a "charitable interpretation [of the convergence hypothesis] would be that global pressures oblige governments to do *something*, but do not determine with any precision exactly what they actually choose to do. So it does not force them to 'do NPM'."

Fourth and finally, administrative reform can be driven by ideas or norms. NPM emerged as the neo-liberal model of administrative reform in the overall neo-liberal "turn" in the UK (Suleiman, 2003). There is also a high degree of similarity between NPM and the

American National Performance Review. NPM rested on the basic idea that markets and market-based models of management should be brought into the public sector. Such reform would increase efficiency, cut costs, and increase "customer satisfaction" (see Hood, 1991; Osborne and Gaebler, 1992). This idea, or set of ideas, shaped administrative reform in the UK and the United States and were later adopted and promoted by international institutions.

The central question which will be addressed in this chapter is to what extent administrative reform in Japan, Sweden and the United States has been propelled by universal notions about the proper role and modus operandi of the public sector, and, conversely, to what extent administrative reform implemented in the three countries can be seen as path-dependent reform. Is recent administrative reform in the three jurisdictions a manifestation of globalization, or has this reform rather progressed along paths which are typical to each of the three countries?

This analysis is more complex than it might appear as NPM has both first and second-order effects on the public sector. Much of administrative reform in Western democracies during the late 1990s and early 2000s was aimed at resolving coordination problems (Pollitt and Bouckaert, 2011). Some of these problems can clearly be related to NPM-style reform; by creating agencies, opening up for internal markets, forging partnerships with societal actors, and decentralizing the public sector, government has set itself up for a massive problem in coordinating policy and administration.

## GLOBALIZATION AND ADMINISTRATIVE TRADITIONS

In the context of administrative reform, globalization is assumed to translate into pressures by transnational institutions on national civil service systems; for instance, OECD's Public Management Group (PUMA) was a powerful advocate of NPM reform in the member countries. The World Bank and the IMF has also pushed for domestic deregulation and public sector market-based reform when offering support to different countries. However, global pressures can also be conveyed more in sotto voce but still be equally influential. For example, the growing importance of voluntary international standards and certifications, often described as "soft laws" (Brunsson and Jacobsson, 1998; Mörth, 2004), has driven national governments to implement reform which ensures compliance with international norms. A case in point is the reorganization of the Swedish audit system in 2003 which previously reported to the government but in order to comply with the recommendations and standards issued by the International Organization of Supreme Audit Institutions (INTOSAI) was reformed so that it now reports both to Parliament and the government.[2]

The core issue as we discuss globalization and administrative reform is that one size does not seem to fit all, yet international institutions have insisted that essentially all countries adopt the NPM model of administrative reform. Market-based reform has proven easier to introduce in some countries—particularly the Anglo-American democracies and the Antipodes (Peters, 2001; Pollitt and Bouckaert, 2011; Pierre, 2011a; Toonen, 2001)—than in others; a pattern which substantiates the role of domestic institutions in adapting global concepts of reform to national normative and structural preconditions. This pattern also suggests that administrative traditions differ significantly between different (types of) countries and that they continue to shape administrative organizations and practices (Jabbra and Dwivedi, 2005; Painter and Peters, 2010).

In the context of globalization, this strategy of administrative reform means that since the United States and the UK were the source countries for market-based administrative reform they faced very little pressure to adapt to global norms. Meanwhile, the *Rechtsstaat* systems (see Pierre, 2011a) of continental Europe, Scandinavia, and Asia were urged to redefine substantial normative elements of their public administration.[3]

## COMPARATIVE ADMINISTRATIVE REFORM

We will now turn out the three case countries to briefly review their administrative reform process with particular attention to the degree to which international influences shaped reform.

### Japan

Most accounts of state modernization projects in Japan take their appropriate point of departure in the Meiji restoration era 1868–1912

(Umegaki, 1988; Westney, 1987). The restoration was nothing short of a comprehensive transformation of the Japanese state and political structures into a moderately democratic state with a modern administrative apparatus. Administrative modernization was guided by an infusion of Western culture into the public administration. The project, as Hoshino (1996:361) points out, "was itself reformist, progressive and universalist"; for centuries, the Japanese have been torn between strengthening the bonds with the rest of Asia or adopting a Western, particularly European, state model. This tension persists to date (Hoshino, 1996:362).

The Meiji restoration represented a distinct step towards adopting a Western or European model of administration. Ito Hirubumi, one of the Meiji oligarchs, was strongly influenced by the Prussian model of military and bureaucratic organization, "which he saw as a route to Western rationality and modernity but also as an alternative to Anglo-Saxon liberalism" (Woo-Cummings, 2005:100). Hirubumi played a key role in making the Prussian-style of bureaucracy "the absolute, unassailable base and center of political power in the state system" (ibid; Woo-Cummings, 1995). Thus, while there was some tension concerning the normative and cultural foundation of the state and its administrative system, the Japanese chose to look to the West for models of administrative organization that could serve as examples for the modernization of the bureaucracy.

Indeed, as Hoshino (1996:360) argues, emulating Western administrative practices and organizations was an important element of modernization as a form of adaptation to the international environment. Administrative reform inspired by overseas administrative systems has a long and continuous history in Japan; a reform strategy that has been conducted on Japan's own terms. During the crisis-ridden 1990s, however, this pattern changed.

Since 1970, but particularly after the oil crisis in the mid-1970s, administrative reform in Japan has been linked to fiscal reform. This was also the time when deregulation was first implemented. Around 1980, deregulation became more closely linked to economic growth. The objective of deregulation now was to "enhance the efficiency of private actors. Given the poor economic condition at that time, public works could not be used to stimulate the economy."[4]

In 1981, Prime Minister Nakasone appointed a Commission on administrative reform called SPARC (Second Provisional Administrative Reform Commission; see Wright and Sakurai,

1987). SPARC launched an extensive reform agenda clearly inspired by the recently elected neo-liberal leaders in the United States and the UK. Between 1987 and 1992, administrative reform included the full range of the public sector, including privatization, decentralization, deregulation, and public finance management. However, while there was now growing attention to administrative reform, the programs adopted during much of the 1980s and early 1990s were never fully implemented. The political commitment to reform was low and it did not require too much bureaucratic opposition to prevent change.[5]

Only 5–6 years later, the picture was almost completely different. Administrative reform was now a top political priority and the Commission charged with authority to lead reform was chaired by Prime Minister Hashimoto (Masujima, 2005). The explanation for this new situation was the rapidly spreading financial crisis (Muramatsu and Matsunami, 2003). By the late 1990s when the full extent of the crisis was visible, public management and administrative reform were atop the political agenda. Once again, the Japanese looked to the West for ideas on how to reform the state. The Hashimoto Commission studied the National Performance Review program and the Government Performance and Result Act (GPRA) in the United States and the Public Service Agreements evaluation in the UK.

Thus it is easy to see the financial crisis as a "punctuated equilibrium" in the administrative reform trajectory. This is also the interpretation offered by Muramatsu and Matsunami (2003) who link the pace and direction of administrative reform directly to the economy. During the high-growth era, the Japanese political and bureaucratic elites could afford some complacency in terms of administrative reform. True, there was reform but it did not address the core problems in the public sector and it lacked senior political support. When the financial crisis, or crises, hit Japan in the 1990s, reform gained massive momentum and support.[6]

Turning now to the substance of reform, the past couple of decades have seen some steps towards decentralization. The Japanese tend to see decentralization as a component of administrative reform. Given the historically high degree of centralization of the Japanese state which places political power in the hands of senior public servants in the central government ministries, decentralization "strikes at the heart of Japanese politics" (Nakamura, 1996:5). As is the case in most countries, but probably only more so in Japan, decentralization is a complicated political project with at least as many enemies as allies. Nonetheless, in 1995 the Diet adopted legislation on "The Promotion of decentralization" and an "omnibus Act of decentralization" was adopted in 1999.[7]

These formal pieces of legislation do not tell the whole story, however. We saw in the previous chapter that political and fiscal decentralization do not always correspond; whereas political and administrative decentralization is sometimes referred to as a "functional rearrangement of government", unfunded mandates seem to be considered routine matters between central and subnational government.

Japan has taken a somewhat reluctant stance towards NPM. The legalistic nature of the Japanese public administration looms large:

> We have to be very incremental. It takes a lot of energy to transform a legalistic system. For instance, in the case of privatization of the postal service (a big issue in the 2005 elections), we have to proceed carefully. We cannot renationalize . . . Political initiatives are necessary for reform. NPM is believed to be popular among many constituencies. Before a tax or fee is introduced, we have to show people how we did our best but did not quite succeed and so we had to introduce a tax.[8]

We mentioned earlier that Japan has a long history of studying foreign countries for ideas on how to design domestic reform. Administrative reform during the past three decades has been shaped by both endogenous and exogenous norms and ideas and the exogenous norms have at times been searched and imported and other times more imposed. To some extent, imposition has aimed at opening up Japanese domestic markets and to implement deregulation, as we saw in Chapter 3. Thus, Muramatsu and Matsunami (2003:176–7) suggest that "deregulation has been more a by-product of US–Japan negotiations than a product of efforts to reform the public sector. The deregulation movement was originally meant to curtail and halt the leadership of the Ministry of International Trade and Industry (MITI) in industrial policies, but deregulation has since come to be associated with the promotion of public sector effectiveness."

Other observers agree that the American insistence on deregulation in Japan was primarily motivated by US trade interests and less a reform intended to improve the efficiency of the Japanese economic system. Kudo (2001:127) thus argues:

> Post-war Japan has often been labelled a land of 'public weakness and private flooding' and certainly it has failed to achieve a national consensus on the relationship between the public and private spheres. If under this condition Japan adopts unadulterated US-style deregulation, then the nation faces the danger of ending up with even more troubles than the US presently faces.

To sum up this brief analysis of Japanese administrative reform, it is a reform process which perhaps is characteristic of a highly centralized system of government enjoying a strong economic growth for decades but then falling into financial crisis. It was difficult to mobilize political support for reform when the economy was doing so exceptionally well. When major problems arose, reform climbed rapidly on the agenda. The crisis enabled reform which probably had not been possible to conduct before, substantively or politically. The Japanese have not hesitated to look at reform in other countries, and some reform was also imposed on the country as part of the support packages offered by the IMF to address the financial crisis.

## Sweden

Administrative reform in Sweden shares a couple of features with the Japanese case. The Swedish bureaucracy has for a long time observed public administration and management in other countries in search of ideas which can be brought into the Swedish administration. More significantly, the deep financial crisis in the early 1990s redefined institutional roles and brought in new models of management and coordination.

One of the paradoxes surrounding administrative reform in Sweden is the combination of a very large public sector, not least in historical (post-Second World War) perspective, on the one hand, and the absence of coordinated programs of reform on the other. This is not to suggest that there was no administrative reform, only that it was conducted with a minimum of discourse and with very little parliamentary oversight. Given the centrality of its extensive welfare state one would suspect that the quality of administration and public service should be a more salient issue than it appears to be. Reform has been conducted with very little political presence and without a comprehensive program defining objectives and means. Thus, administrative reform was to a very large extent driven and designed by the bureaucracy itself. This has not meant that the reform process was slow or autopoietic; on the contrary, senior civil servants explored the international environment in search of organizational and managerial models that could serve as templates for domestic reform.

There is one exception to the observation that Sweden has not had a program of administrative reform. This followed on the 1976 election, placing the Social Democrats in opposition for the first time in more than four decades. The main opposition party, The Center Party, campaigned on a platform emphasizing decentralization and secured support from about 25 percent of the electorate. While in opposition the Social Democrats produced an administrative reform program aiming at deregulation, empowering clients vis-à-vis the bureaucracy, and increasing service and transparency (Gustafsson and Svensson, 1999). The program, implemented during the 1980s, could easily be seen as a response to the electoral defeat (Pierre, 1993).

However, we can see several examples of more piecemeal administrative reform even further back in time. During the expansion of welfare state programs and the public bureaucracy that went with them in the 1960s and 1970s, the steadily increasing tax pressure became a sensitive issue to the government. There was a need to develop instruments to monitor and evaluate the spending of public financial resources. As a result, Swedish bureaucrats went on study trips in the late 1960s and 1970s to the United States to learn about program budgeting and brought ideas home with them. They also participated in evaluation research conferences in the United States and Europe, for example the European Group of Evaluation Research and the American equivalent of that organization. A group of civil servants at the then National Audit Office (RRV) were frequent visitors to PUMA and the European Group for Public Administration (EGPA) conferences.

Thus, the basic concepts, methods, and techniques of (at that time) modern public administration came from the outside world and became key components of domestic administrative reform (Niklasson and Pierre, 2012; Sundström, 2003). The basic features of performance measurement were also imported this way and there was close collaboration between Sweden and Canada in the 1980s on issues related to performance management. Indeed, "Sweden was the first country to develop annual result analyses. They appeared a few years later in the United States."[9]

There was a strong tendency among senior bureaucrats during the 1970s and 1980s to look at countries like the United States and the UK for guidance on how to curb public expenditure. At the same time, practitioners were weary of advocating a wholesale import of NPM. As a senior staff member at the Swedish National Financial Management Authority argues:

> We never really believed in [NPM] here. There never was an explicit decision made concerning the adoption of NPM as a model of administrative reform. There were bits and pieces of NPM which we used or still use in Sweden—management by objectives or management by results, delegated authority, three-year budget cycle all came and went—but this was something we did long before NPM. This was the established Swedish modus operandi which had been in practice since long before PUMA and NPM.[10]

There has been a strong continuity in Sweden in the way administrative reform has been defined and debated, from the days of program budgeting onwards. Sweden has not adopted NPM as a strategy to reduce the power of the state. The "bits and pieces of NPM" mentioned by the practitioner above have however left their mark on the public administration. Management by objectives and results still defines much of the relationship between government departments and the agencies. Performance measurement and management have been extensively implemented, so much so that the past several years have seen a debate about whether performance management has a detrimental effect on public service design. Furthermore, competitive tendering is today exercised in a wide range of public service areas. And, there has been a "choice revolution" in service delivery as public monopolies in health care and primary education and other sectors have been replaced by markets where public and private service providers compete (Blomqvist, 2004). While it remains true that NPM has not been introduced to a large extent, the observation is more valid for the national public administration than for service delivery at the local government level. This becomes a complex matter in a country with a developed welfare state which emphasizes equal treatment, transparency, legal security, and the rule of law. Miller and Rose (2008:105) argue that implementing

NPM in the Scandinavian welfare states means that "the logics of welfare bureaucracies are replaced by new logics of competition". The Scandinavian societies are state-centric. It is difficult to change the structure or the modus operandi of the state in such societies without challenging popular perceptions of the state.

International influences have thus been integral to administrative reform. Those influences have overwhelmingly been sought rather than imposed. Reform has been designed by the bureaucracy itself with very little political interference or leadership. The result of this technocratic model of reform has been that overseas ideas have been incorporated into the Swedish public administration without any other considerations than their feasibility to solve the problems at hand.

## The United States

In the early fall of 2008 when the first section of field work was done for this study, there was some unease among the public management consultancies along K Street in Washington, DC With the Presidential election just a couple of months away, much of the business was on hold. The only thing certain was that the next President would launch an agenda for administrative and public management reform, but no one had a clue as to what "the next thing" would be.

Paul Light (1997) has showed how each new presidential administration tends to make their mark in the administrative reform trajectory. Although every administration adopts its own program there can still be significant similarities with the program of the previous administration. The past couple of decades have seen two eight-year periods of reform; first the 1992–2000 Clinton era featuring the National Performance Review (henceforth NPR) and the "reinventing government" process, then the 2000–2008 George W. Bush program PMA (President's Management Agenda).

NPR was in many ways reflective of the private sector with its emphasis on customer orientation, empowerment of lower-level employees, markets in public service delivery, reduced supervision, and a search for excellence (U.S. National Performance Review, 1993; see also Osborne and Gaebler, 1992). The program included all essential elements of the public administration; its management, staff, client relations, and structure. It was also about budget-cutting and deregulation. Assessments suggest that it was not altogether successful, given its far-reaching objectives (Kettl, 1994; Thompson, 2000). NPR was however to a large extent a bottom-up process and the states were ahead of the federal administration in the reform process (Brudney et al., 1999).

PMA, launched in August 2001, had a focus on management reform in the civil service, including financial management. There was also an emphasis on the development of e-government. "These issues had been talked about beforehand and were already underway; it was a repackaging of ideas already on the agenda."[11]

Human resource (HR) management reform in the federal civil service has aimed at deregulation (e.g. removing the FPM, the 10,000-page Federal Personnel Manual), decentralization and delegation of management tasks to line managers. NPR-based reform in the HR management in the federal civil service was extensive; the Office of Personnel Management (OPM) was basically cut in half (Ban, 1998:28). Drivers of reform (see Ban, 1998; Kettl, 1994) have been drastic cuts in agency budgets with subsequent reduction in staff. Furthermore, new technology has driven administrative reform, for instance in HR management. Third, there has been a strong emphasis on customer service and "strategic human resource management".

There appears to have been extremely limited international influences on administrative reform in the United States. Going over reform documents, secondary literature, and listening to interviewees provides a consistent account of an almost complete absence of any visible overseas influences on the US administrative reform. Carolyn Ban's detailed analysis of the drivers of reform in the HR management sector never mentions international influences or overseas leading examples. One of the interviewees put it rather bluntly:

> Call it myopia or arrogance but we believe that it all ends here. The fact that someone else has done it has no bearing here . . . We look at the US experience but there are some features you can not learn from state and local governments. For instance, with regard to health care and national security there is nothing we can learn from states and cities. We also observe what happens in some other countries like Canada, Belgium and Sweden but it has no real impact on our reform. It is not a matter of 'monkey see, monkey do' . . . The United States had no use for NPM. Some ideas from Australia and New Zealand gained some attention but they were only instructive. Australia, the UK, and New Zealand had much more to privatize. There was nothing for us to learn.[12]

Another interviewee with extensive experience of working in the US federal service argued along similar lines: "The United States federal government is really very insulate. The thinking can be quite parochial. In terms of international influences we in the United States do not think that way . . . Cultural differences between the U.S. and other countries are believed to be bigger than differences between the public and private sector in the United States."[13]

This is probably not to say that reform designers never reflected on how similar issues were addressed in other countries—Al Gore was said to have been inspired by the Next Steps program in the UK—but it is indicative of the seemingly oblivious role of international points of reference in US administrative reform. Indeed, the US process of administrative reform and the American oblivion to the rest of the world in this respect echoes Judge Brandeis' famous ruling in 1932 that "a state may, if its citizens choose, serve as a laboratory; and try novel social and economic experiments without risk to the rest of the country".[14]

Indeed, it appears as if administrative reform has been more influenced by management ideas in the domestic corporate sector than in the public sector of other countries (see Allison, 1986). In 1982, President Reagan appointed the Grace Commission, comprised by a group of senior business leaders, to investigate the problem of low public sector inefficiency. Looking to the corporate sector and markets for models of management and client (or customer) orientation, a reform concept often associated with NPR (or NPM), had thus been practiced for some time in America:

> Adopting ideas and strategies from the private sector is sometime in vogue. Much depends on how well the private sector is doing. NPR was clearly influenced by the private sector. The legality of the public sector is not really an obstacle to adopting ideas from the private sector. The private sector too has a lot of laws and regulations, for instance for hiring and firing, affirmative action, and so on.[15]

To summarize, the US case of administrative reform, NPR and the "reinvention" campaign created a powerful momentum for reform which, although the program was not fully implemented, has had substantive impact on the US public administration. International influences have been minimal. Instead the private sector has served as somewhat of a role model for management and client relations. What could be seen as a parochial philosophy of reform could also be interpreted as reform being designed in accordance with the actual problems and not being imposed from the outside thus leading to inconsistencies and "institutional friction" (Steinmo, 2012).

## CONCLUDING COMMENTS

The globalization argument in the context of administrative reform posits that countries are converging in their administrative reform. The competing hypothesis states that although there is reform, critical systemic differences persist. In all three case countries, administrative reform has been on the agenda for the past 25 years or more and the types of reform that have been implemented have indicated a breach and new direction of the reform trajectory. We might expect these new directions to be related to NPM, given that this reform model has been so strongly endorsed by major international institutions like the IMF, the World Bank, the WTO, and the OECD.

Interestingly, however, none of the three case countries have implemented NPM reform to a major extent. In Japan there has been some such reform, for example deregulation, privatization, and the creation of autonomous agencies. However, much of this reform was set in motion prior to the global diffusion of market-driven managerial reform. In some cases, reform was part of US–Japan trade negotiations where America sought to remove regulation which was said to serve mainly as barriers to trade. In other cases, deregulation is conducted in order to increase market efficiency. In Sweden, NPM reforms preceded the NPM campaign by a couple of decades; it was driven by problems of performance measurement and control of public spending. In the United States, finally—as was vehemently pointed out in interviews—extensive market-based reform has been introduced across the board albeit not under the NPM banner but as part of the NPR and the "reinventing government" programs.

Table 5.1 gives a summary of administrative reform in the three countries.

In Japan, administrative reform is seen as subordinate to economic growth and reform seeks to develop the civil service into an optimal institutional tool towards that end. At the same time, however, market regulation has helped insulate the domestic economy from overseas competition. In the United States, the main drivers of change have been bureaucratic rigidities, low efficiency, and high

*Table 5.1 Administrative reform in Japan, Sweden, and the United States*

| | 1980s | 1990s | 2000s |
|---|---|---|---|
| Japan | Privatization<br>Deregulation | Regulatory reform<br>Deregulation | Decentralization |
| Sweden | Renewal of the public sector, decentralization, deregulation | Budget cuts, "purification"<br>Management by objectives and results | Market-based reform<br>Performance management |
| USA | Grace Commission<br>Budget cuts, financial management | National Performance Review<br>Reinvention | Performance management |

costs in service delivery and there has been a strong tendency to emulate private sector management models to address those issues. Sweden presents yet another model. There, administrative reform has a more multidimensional appearance. Certainly, in a country with the historically biggest public sector in the Western world and one of the highest tax pressures, cutting costs and increasing efficiency become important objectives almost by default. Historically, and with an imperfect timeline, it could be argued that Japan has been inspired by European models of administration; Sweden has adopted reform ideas from the United States; while US reform has emulated the private sector at home.

Cutting costs has been important in all three countries but the strategies to achieve that goal have differed. All countries have introduced or expanded market-based reform to help increase efficiency and cut costs, but they have done so through different processes. Thus while there is some convergence among the three case countries in these respects, that convergence is explained more by similarities in the problems facing governments than global imposition of norms and values. The only exceptions to this pattern would be the pressures exerted on Japan bilaterally by the US and by the IMF during the financial crisis and the OECD's insistence that Japan, but also Sweden, introduce market-based administrative reform.

If thus the globalization hypothesis is largely rejected, the competing path-dependent hypothesis, too, receives little support. The three cases suggest that there is indeed domestic choice in the field of administrative reform and that in some countries that choice has been exercised to launch new paths in administrative reform. This is most clearly the case in the United States where NPR defined a new path in administrative reform in so far as it introduced a new philosophy for public service organization and production. In Japan, the financial crisis in the 1990s punctuated the equilibrium in administrative reform and opened up for new ideas and programs. So far only rather limited NPM-style reform has been implemented, partly because NPM does not offer a significant contribution to economic development and partly because of the tensions between NPM and the legalistic administrative tradition in Japan. In Sweden, finally, there has been more NPM-type administrative reform—some of it preceding the global NPM campaign by several decades—but not sufficient to call the Swedish administrative tradition into question.

In all three countries, it is safe to say that their respective bureaucracies of the twenty-first century look significantly different from those of, say, the 1960s or 1970s. There are similarities in the direction of change but not enough to sustain a convergence thesis or a globalization thesis. They wrestle with similar issues and problems and apply rather similar approaches to those problems. With a few and important exceptions, global pressures have not been able to alter the course of reform. It is only in times of crisis that the integrity of domestic choice is compromised and overseas pressures become difficult to resist.

## NOTES

1. In the US reform vernacular, market-based reform is referred to not as NPM but as National Performance Review (NPR) and "reinvention of government". NPM is seen as typical to the UK, Australia, and New Zealand.
2. There were also domestic pressures for the reorganization, too; not least that Parliament needed a powerful auditing institution.
3. "*Rechtsstaat*" is German, meaning in translation "a state governed under the law".
4. Senior official and Cabinet Office member of staff, Administrative Promotion Office, Ministry of Internal Affairs and Communications, October 24, 2005.
5. Senior official and Cabinet Office member of staff, Administrative Promotion Office, Ministry of Internal Affairs and Communications, October 24, 2005. See also Muramatsu and Matsunami (2003:174).
6. In contrast to this perspective, a senior bureaucrat offered the view that the bursting of the bubble in the economy and the ensuing financial turmoil had no impact on administrative reform: "Administrative reform has always been consequential. Reform began already in the early 1980s and there has been a straight line in administrative reform since then. The Second Provisional Administrative Reform Council was created in 1981. Today's reform path can be traced back to that time." Senior official and Cabinet Office member of staff, Administrative Promotion Office, Ministry of Internal Affairs and Communications, October 24, 2005.
7. The concept of the "Omnibus" Act means that it contained instructions on decentralization in several different policy sectors.
8. Senior official and Cabinet Office member of staff, Administrative Promotion Office, Ministry of Internal Affairs and Communications, October 24, 2005. Note that taxes are seen as administrative failures.
9. Senior official, Swedish National Financial Management Authority, June 12, 2008.
10. Senior official, Swedish National Financial Management Authority, October 17, 2007. See Niklasson and Pierre, 2012; Sundström, 2003.
11. Consultant and former deputy Director in the US federal service, September 2, 2008.
12. Executive Director for major consultancy, September 3, 2008.
13. Consultant and former deputy Director in the US federal service, September 2, 2008.

14. *New State Ice Company* vs. *Liebmann* (1932). I owe this observation to Guy Peters.
15. Consultant and former deputy Director in the US federal service, September 2, 2008.

# 6. Conclusions: domestic governance in a globalizing world

Globalization itself is neither good nor bad.
Joseph Stiglitz, 2003

The usual understanding of a dichotomy between the state and globalisation is an illusion, as the processes of global restructuring are largely embedded within state structures and institutions, politically contingent on state policies and actions, and primarily about the reorganisation of the state.
Amoore et al., 1997:186

In this concluding chapter we first summarize our results country by country. Throughout this book we have argued that the degree to which nation states adopt or resist global norms and reform ideas is explained first and foremost by domestic political, institutional, economic and cultural factors. These factors are, for the most part, "inert" variables that change only incrementally and would therefore appear to provide very little explanatory capacity in the short-term perspective. The perspective applied in this book takes a more long-term view on the impact of globalization, thus allowing us to see the effects of, for example, changes in key economic parameters.

We will then cut the pie the other way and look at our findings sector by sector to search for cross-national commonalities in governance reform. What are the main similarities and differences between reforms in the three countries and how can we account for those patterns?

We close the chapter by returning to the discussion in the introductory chapter on the past century as "the American century".

## THREE CASES, THREE STORYLINES OF GLOBALIZATION

The three countries that we have chosen as cases for our analysis present three different accounts of the impact of globalization. The reader is reminded that they are all affluent, advanced democracies and their experiences do not speak to those of the developing countries.

### Japan

Japan has a long history with internationalization. The country has never been averse to incorporating ideas from overseas. From the Meiji restoration in the 1880s (perhaps even further back in time) onwards, Japan has observed how issues similar to those confronting the Japanese society have been resolved elsewhere, for instance in the areas of administrative modernization or macroeconomic policy (Westney, 1987; Woo-Cummings, 2005). Its international embeddedness is furthermore demonstrated by its performance in overseas markets which provided the economic base for the economic recovery after the Second World War. Japan is however struggling to become an integrated member of the international community, for instance as a participant in peace-keeping missions and other UN-sponsored international actions. Indeed, Japan's stature in international politics is nowhere near its economic prominence in world markets (Soeya et al., 2011).

The first couple of decades after the Second World War saw Japan excelling in a strategy of protecting its domestic markets from overseas competition while at the same time bringing home huge export revenues. Economic growth is seen as the foundation for national independence and autonomy and therefore takes precedence in domestic politics (Johnson, 1982). Accordingly, economic governance, administrative reform, and inter-governmental relationships are conducted in ways which produce the biggest contribution to sustained economic development.

The financial crisis during the 1990s changed to a large extent this state of affairs. Japan now faced growing difficulties in conducting its relationships with its environment on its own terms and economic growth came to a standstill. Instead of carefully managing the process of adopting reform ideas from overseas, such ideas were now imposed on Japan by international financial institutions. Some reform concepts, for instance deregulation reform, had been underway for some time but were now given priority. Other elements of reform had a more profound impact on the Japanese economy; this was particularly the case with changes in the regulatory framework of industrial ownership which eliminated much of the coordination of Japanese industry.

Japan thus describes a trajectory from a position of mastering the economic dimensions of globalization towards growing contingencies on global financial institutions and having to deal with global pressures. The strategy of "permeable insulation" (Schaede and Grimes, 2003b) is predicated on a fair degree of state control over economic and political transactions across its borders. The financial instabilities during the latter part of the 1990s and the insufficient governance mechanisms available to address the crisis made it extremely difficult for the government to sustain "permeable insulation"; permeability increased, insulation decreased, and instead of proactively engaging her environment Japan had little choice but to react to the directives from that environment.

## Sweden

Like Japan, Sweden has a long history in accommodating international economic challenges. The adaptive capacity appears to have been lower than in Japan, in part because the institutional system is more decentralized and in part because of the role of powerful organized interests with access to the policy process. It is true, as Katzenstein argues, that corporatism is not just an obstacle to reform but in fact a vehicle for reform; it provides a system of domestic compensation in national economies with strong trade dependencies (Katzenstein, 1984, 1985). However, alongside globalization we have seen a partial decline in corporatism in the Scandinavian countries. Interestingly, recent studies find no correlation between real-wage compensation and the degree of trade openness within the OECD group of countries (Pain and Koske, 2007). That pattern might suggest that domestic politics in the traditionally corporatist systems has developed from a Keynesian-style economic policy with significant distributive elements to compensate constituencies exposed to international competition towards a stricter neo-liberal economic regime emphasizing economic balance and restrictive distributive policies.

The trajectory of economic development in Sweden would fit that description. Following a deep financial crisis in the early 1990s, maintaining macroeconomic balance became a top political priority. Economic governance has been redesigned towards that goal. The National Bank has been given a more autonomous role in relation to the political leadership and the Department of Finance has significantly increased its control over public expenditure and policies which might drive such expenditure. Policy objectives like national competitiveness, deregulating markets, support of research and development, stimulating foreign direct investment, and cutting taxes and public expenditure have moved upward on the political agenda.

These developments have not come easy as the welfare state has strong political and electoral support. Administrative reform to boost efficiency in service delivery has therefore emerged as a critical component of the larger policy reassessment and change. Many of these reforms were implemented or underway prior to the global New Public Management campaign. The 1992 financial crisis served as a strong catalyst for administrative reform towards public management.

It would thus appear as if Sweden gradually has transformed itself to the globalized economy and that the transformation, with the important exception of the financial crisis, was driven more by endogenous than exogenous forces. Joining the EU in 1996 opened up the Swedish government, administration, and subnational governments to new regulatory frameworks and provided opportunities to mobilize new types of financial and other resources.

## United States

The cases of Japan and Sweden highlight the complexities of accommodating global or international pressures. The United States' experience in that respect looks rather different. In economic governance, the NAFTA agreement signifies the widespread tendency to build regional free-trade zones. Convinced that doing so was in the long-term interests of the American economy, President Bush and later President Clinton committed themselves strongly to the agreement and the accommodation of domestic constituencies affected by the expanded free-trade area.

Economic governance is characterized by the huge domestic

market and a moderate political presence in the economy. The 1980s and 1990s witnessed a series of deregulation reform in the transportation, energy, communication, and financial markets. This reform, and indeed most of economic governance, was conducted with a minimum of external pressures.

The same pattern applies to administrative reform where the trajectory of reform suggests that more inspiration was sought in the domestic private sector than in the public sector of other countries. Reform may have been inspired by events overseas but not driven, let alone imposed, by exogenous institutions or actors.

Inter-governmental relationships in the United States has not been an area of federally initiated reform, neither in terms of internationalization nor in governance. Local government and urban governance is slowly modernizing, as we saw earlier. Reforms like local government mergers which have been implemented in Japan and Sweden are not on the agenda.

The general pattern from these areas of governance is that reform—sometimes far-reaching and innovative reform as was the case with the National Performance Review and "reinvention" reform in the administrative reform sector—is certainly implemented, but international factors play an extremely limited role in the process. Reform is not imposed by international institutions, nor is it influenced by reform in other countries. Globalization may have had a moderate effect on subnational internationalization. Globalization has not hit the American society and economy the same way it impacted rather dramatically on the two other case countries.

The architects of reform in the United States appear to be convinced that the rest of the world has very little to offer in terms of ideas and practices that could be inserted into the reform process. At the state and local levels there is ample opportunity to learn from other institutions within the same national context. The corporate sector serves as a role model for public management and public sector reform more broadly. This strategy of reform minimizes the risks of adopting models from overseas jurisdictions which may later turn out to be unsuited for the American public sector. Thus there is learning, but only within the system.

## THREE SECTORS OF REFORM

### Economic Governance

The three countries have all experienced severe financial crises. Furthermore, all three countries, but Japan and Sweden in particular, have lengthy experience of adjusting to changes in international markets. Economic governance is a competitive instrument; countries that develop efficient governance of their economy will foster a competitive businesses sector.

Obviously, different countries and types of economy hold different views about how that goal is achieved and what role the government should take in enhancing competitiveness (Hall and Soskice, 2001). Japan, Sweden, and the United States present three different national strategies in this respect. Japan and Sweden, both typical of Hall and Soskice's "coordinated market economy" model, have historically accorded the state a leading and coordinating role in the economy. In the US there is much more emphasis on the market as the key source of competitiveness and the role of the state is mainly to provide regulatory frameworks.

Economic governance reform has not altered these fundamental features of the three economies although the Japanese and Swedish political economies have undergone some change. Sweden is gradually transforming towards a more market-based economy; tax levels and the size of the public sector are now more in line with those of Sweden's main competitors although there is still significant regulatory intervention in the market. Japan, too, has seen profound changes in its economy, not least as a part of an increasing foreign ownership and in the degree of cross-ownership (see Chapter 3).

It could thus be fair to say that there has been some convergence among the three economies in the sense that the Japanese and Swedish economies have partially adopted some of the neo-liberal features of the US political economy. In the case of Japan, these changes are to some degree related to changes in ownership structure and Japan's post-crisis concessions in international agreements. For Sweden, changes in the economy can mainly be related to the economic policy reassessments after the troublesome early 1990s. Indeed, financial crises have been integral to these changes in Japan and Sweden while the 2008 crisis in the US financial system seems to have had less dramatic domestic political ramifications. The accommodation of the crisis and the more long-term adjustments to prevent future crises drove the Japanese and Swedish liberalization processes.

## Inter-governmental Relationships

The main (direct or indirect) impact of globalization on inter-governmental relationships has been rescaling; the relaxation of the domestic institutional hierarchy and the incentives and opportunities it meant for cities to develop international networks and partnerships. This pattern is quite clear in Japan and Sweden. It is also the case for many of the bigger US cities and cities close to national borders, although generally speaking internationalization is a less salient project among US local governments compared to Japanese or Swedish cities.

Rescaling is tied to globalization but through more complex processes than being merely a global imperative for cities and regions to "go international". Domestic institutional politics, for example the reduced central government support to cities and regions and the increasing tendency for the state to give subnational government unfunded mandates, explains to a large extent why cities and regions began to explore international arenas. In the case of Sweden, the EU membership triggered subnational internationalization on a large scale.

## Administrative Reform

Perhaps contrary to expectations, administrative reform is the sector where we have found the fewest cases of global drivers of reform. Only in Japan has administrative (NPM) reform been imposed by exogenous actors or institutions. Reform in Sweden has been as extensive as in Japan but has been more path-dependent; public management reform can be traced back several decades in time. In the United States reform has continuously been inspired by corporate models of organization, management, and client orientation.

The three countries vary considerably with regard to how extensively they have introduced NPM (or, in the case of the United States, NPR) reform. The US federal government launched an extensive program which was never fully implemented at the federal level but more so at the state level. Japan and Sweden, both with

*Rechtsstaat* administrative traditions, were more tentative towards market-based administrative reform and implementation therefore has been slower and more limited than in the United States.

Table 6.1 summarizes the main findings of the study. For each of the nine case studies, we assess firstly whether the sources of reform have been endogenous or exogenous, or both; secondly, we describe the extent of reform as moderate or extensive; and thirdly, we indicate whether the case supports the globalization hypothesis or the path dependency hypothesis.

Table 6.1 shows that globalization and international influences have been most noticeable in the three sectors of Japanese governance. In Sweden, economic governance and inter-governmental relationships have been influenced by globalization. For both countries, the financial crisis represented a "punctuated equilibrium" in economic governance. In the US, none of the three governance sectors have been significantly influenced by exogenous factors. We will return to this observation in the final section of the chapter.

## GLOBALIZATION AND THE STATE

What do these findings tell us about the relationship between global drivers of change on the one hand and the resilience of the state on the other? Four general conclusions which speak to the theoretical analysis of these issues come out of the study.

First, the globalization argument is static and underestimates the learning capacity of the state. Sweden learned during the 1990s that an economy featuring a fixed currency exchange rate, bubble tendencies, and increasing deficits and debt is susceptible to international speculation. Since then, budgetary and fiscal control and a restored balance in the economy have been top political priorities. In a similar way, Japan reformed the regulatory framework of its financial system after the deep financial crisis during the 1990s. Like other Asian countries, Japan has been characteristically pragmatic in adopting ideas from other countries and inserting them into its domestic reform process. Thus, over time governments have become better at understanding the logic of a globalized, deregulated economy and its consequences for the domestic economy.

The United States presents a different case in this respect. As we have seen, there appears to be very limited interest in learning

*Table 6.1 Globalization and path dependency in economic governance, intergovernmental relationships, and administrative reform in Japan, Sweden, and the United States: Summary of main results*

| | **Japan** | **Sweden** | **United States** |
|---|---|---|---|
| Economic governance | Endogenous and exogenous drivers<br>Extensive reform<br>Globalization | Endogenous and exogenous drivers<br>Extensive reform<br>Globalization | Endogenous drivers<br>Moderate reform<br>Path dependency |
| Intergovernmental relationships | Endogenous and exogenous drivers<br>Extensive reform<br>Globalization | Endogenous and exogenous drivers<br>Extensive reform<br>Globalization | Endogenous drivers<br>Moderate reform<br>Path dependency |
| Administrative reform | Endogenous and exogenous drivers<br>Extensive reform<br>Globalization | Endogenous drivers<br>Extensive reform<br>Path dependency | Endogenous drivers<br>Extensive reform<br>Path dependency |

how other countries address problems which may be quite similar to those confronting US politicians and bureaucrats. If anything, there is rather a philosophy that the United States has very little to learn from such studies. Interviewees acknowledge—in an almost *sui generis* mode of reasoning—that their views may be myopic and parochial but, even so, they insist that there are no countries that experience quite the same problems that the United States is facing. Instead, learning takes place within the system, among states or local governments.

Secondly, we have found that similarities among different countries may be the outcome of similar problems rather than the result of global pressures. Most governments today face problems related to economic growth, an ageing population, increasing costs in service delivery, migration, national security, and so on. Some similarity in terms of policy and governance should therefore only be expected. That said, similarities among different countries could also be related to the role of international pressures. The diffusion of New Public Management reform, promoted by the OECD, the World Bank, and the IMF, is a case in point. The argument here is simply that all similarities in state behavior cannot be taken as proof of global pressures on national governments.

Third, the globalization argument underestimates the diversity of national contexts. As many observers on globalization agree, the impact of globalization on the state depends just as much on domestic factors as on the nature of the global pressures. States with a solid economy and strong, insulated institutions are in a better position to oppose global influences compared to states suffering from an unbalanced economy and insufficient institutional integrity. Japan could defer of fend off pressures (bilateral or multilateral) on its domestic regulatory frameworks and governance for decades because it had the necessary financial and institutional capabilities to do so. Japan was anxious not to disturb its relationship with its ally the United States but it was not needy for support from international financial institutions. When the financial crisis uncovered major flaws in its economic governance and placed the state in acute dependency on international support, Japan's autonomy was jeopardized. Sweden's situation during its financial turmoil presented similar problems of a short-term loss of control and autonomy. The United States has had a tendency to both create and solve its financial crises in-house and has therefore not been equally exposed to the conditioned imperatives of international institutions. Thus, countries differ both diachronically and synchronically with respect to their capacity to resist international political or economic pressures.

Fourth and finally, global ideas cannot penetrate nation–state border unless they are promoted by powerful carriers. They may provide national governments with advice, sometimes even emphatic advice, and they may catalyze domestic reform but they are not often the main driver of domestic reform. Again, this pattern is broken during states' financial crises when ideas are brought into domestic choice as part of the rescue package provided by international financial institutions.

We also note that globalization and path dependency might appear to be an awkward conceptual juxtaposition as "punctuated equilibriums" can be the result of domestic factors as well as international factors. The path dependency hypothesis does not exclude the possibility of extensive reform as long as it is consistent with the long-term trajectory of development. That said, administrative reform in the United States and Sweden could be described as being given a new direction when the NPR campaign was launched in 1990s in the US and performance management was introduced in the 1960s and 1970s in Sweden.

## GLOBALIZATION AND AMERICANIZATION

Following the 2008 financial crisis, Robert Altman reflected in an article in *Foreign Affairs* on the consequences of the crisis on world politics and globalization (Altman, 2009b). Globalization was now in retreat, he argues. The downfall of the crisis has seen regions and groups of international leaders failing to launch a coordinated strategy to address the economic downturn. "This coincides with the movement away from a unipolar world, which the downturn has accelerated. The United States will now be focused inward and constrained by unemployment and fiscal pressures. Much of the world also blames U.S. financial excesses for the global recession. This has put the U.S. model of free-market capitalism out of favor." Altman was also concerned by the fact that "economic divergence is increasing".

Altman's reflections are indicative of an America-centric model of globalization as essentially a universal adoption of an American model of capitalism. The model also assumes American uni-polar leadership. Globalization has drawn on and reinforced American global hegemony (see, for instance, Ikenberry, 2007; Kudo, 2001). As a result, the United States itself has had to make significantly smaller concessions or adaptations to external influences in its domestic governance than most other countries, not least Japan and Sweden.

In administrative reform, economic governance, and inter-governmental relationships, American observers insist that the US has had very little to learn from other countries and has had few incentives to adopt models of governance from overseas. Globalization, in this perspective, is about the rest of the world adopting US values, a US economic system, and a US lifestyle. Apart from a general notion of democracy, the only aspect of the United States that has not been promoted internationally is the US system of governance.

The defining feature of a globalized economy—a volatile investment capital offering significant opportunities for economic growth but at the same time expecting short-term returns on investment—is reminiscent of the Anglo-American "liberal market" model of capitalism. There are very few, if any, elements of a "coordinated market economy", that is, the model of capitalism found in Continental Europe, the Scandinavian countries, and several of the bigger Asian economies (Hall and Soskice, 2001). Again, the United States has not had to conduct any major changes in its economic system to ensure American competitiveness in the global economy since that economy rests on norms and objectives which are to a large extent a mirror image of those sustaining the American economy.

If much of globalization is, in fact, Americanization—a global adaptation of US norms and objectives related to economic regulation, administrative reform and free markets—it would appear as if globalization has catered to American interests and that the United States would have a competitive edge over countries that have gone through a complex process of implementing policies and institutional arrangements similar to the ones the US has had for a very long period of time. Previous chapters have suggested that governance reform in the United States has emulated existing models and arrangements in other countries to a much lesser extent than has been the case in Japan and Sweden. The American capacity, and inclination, to learn from other countries has been extremely limited.

A country's capacity to reform itself is related to its learning capacity. Thus, flexibility and adaptive capacity are essential for the state to mitigate the challenges of globalization while exploiting its opportunities. In that respect the US is in no better position than other countries, rather to the contrary. In fact, one could argue that the American state is less capable of adjusting to new circumstances compared to the smaller, industrialized democracies in Europe or even major industrial countries like Korea or Japan where dealing with change has more or less always been part of the daily political decision-making. As a transmitter, far more than a receiver, of global political and economic norms, the US has an awkward relationship with policy and governance ideas in practice overseas. The paradox of hegemony is thus that the hegemon itself, having defined the rules of the game for decades if not centuries, faces significant problems in learning how to adapt to changes in global norms and a more multi-polar global economy and community.

Joseph Nye argues that the paradox of American power is that it is strong enough not to be challenged by anyone yet not sufficiently strong to reach its goals without cooperation with other countries (Nye, 2003). If we accept Nye's argument, such cooperation will inevitably involve some degree of concession by the United States towards an international regime, something which raises the question of its capacity to adjust or learn or adapt to exogenous norms. It might be the case that the 1900s was "the American century" until globalization emerged, and certainly as the biggest economy and sole superpower the United States remains an extremely powerful international actor. However, globalization has opened up international arenas not just for American actors but also for Asian regions and the EU. When other countries have adapted to the global economy, globalization might lead towards increasing multi-polarity, economically and politically.

# Appendix

## THE JAPANESE SAMPLE

The Japanese questionnaire was conducted in 2006 by the Toshi Center in Tokyo. The sample consisted of all local government designated as cities, a total of 725 local governments. 488 responses were received, equal to a response rate of 67.3 percent.

## THE SWEDISH SAMPLE

The Swedish questionnaire was conducted in 2006 by staff at the University of Gothenburg. The sample consisted of all 290 local governments. 209 responses were received, equal to a response rate of 72.1 percent.

## THE US SAMPLE

The US questionnaire was conducted in 2006 by staff at the University of Pittsburgh. The sample was drawn from the membership directory of the International City/County Managers Association (ICMA). ICMA has a good coverage of city and county managers in the United States and its database provides data about the respective city of the managers. That allowed us to compile a sample which would have a representative spread across cities of varying population sizes. From the ICMA membership directory, all of the members from cities with a population of 50,000 residents or more were contacted by mail, or where available by email. In addition a randomized sample of cities with a population of 50,000 or less was drawn (see Table A.1). In total a sample of 2457 city managers were identified. A random selection of case within each cohort was done by SPSS.

*Table A.1 Characteristics of the American sample*

| City size (population) | ICMA membership | Sample | n |
|---|---|---|---|
| >200,000 | 551 | 100% | 551 |
| 100,000–200,000 | 457 | 100% | 457 |
| 50,000–100,000 | 725 | 100% | 725 |
| <50,000 | 3644 | 20% | 727 |

In total 2457 surveys were sent out, and 2167 surveys successfully reached their destination (290 surveys were returned due to wrong addresses or city managers who were no longer in that position). A total of 694 surveys were completed, equal to a 32 percent response rate.

## QUESTIONNAIRE FOR LOCAL AUTHORITIES

**Q1. How would you describe the development of the local economy over the past several years?**
Response alternatives:

1. Improved considerably
2. Improved somewhat
3. Deteriorated somewhat
4. Deteriorated considerably
5. No change

**Q2. How important would you say that these revenue sources are to your city?**
a. Residents' tax
b. Property taxes
c. Service fees
d. General subsidies from the federal government
e. Ear-marked subsidies from the federal government
f. Grants and subsidies from the state government
g. Local loans (bonds)

For each of these items, response alternatives are:

1. Becoming more important
2. Becoming less important
3. Has always been important
4. Has never been important
5. Irrelevant

**Q3. Below are a couple of different strategies for local and regional development listed. Please indicate to which extent they are considered important or unimportant in your city.**

a. Joint projects or partnerships with cities in other countries
b. Partnership with the local business community
c. Bringing in NPOs in the delivery of public service
d. Contracting out of service production and delivery
e. Cooperation with the state
f. Cooperation with other local authorities

For each of these items, response alternatives are:

1. Becoming more important
2. Becoming less important
3. Has always been important
4. Has never been important
5. Irrelevant

**Q4. Which are the main challenges and problems confronting the city today?**

a. Protecting the local environment
b. Declining local tax base
c. Citizens' expectations on the local public services
d. Increasing unemployment
e. Increasing number of elderly people in the city
f. Declining local industries
g. Ethnic diversity and increasing immigration
h. Weak political leadership
i. Problems with inefficiencies in service production
j. Increasing wages for the city employees
k. Many local authorities are too small to be able to deliver good public services (necessity of municipal merger)

l. Declining financial support from the federal government and the state
m. Increasing crime rate

For each of these items, response alternatives are:

1. Major problem
2. Minor problem
3. Not a problem
4. Irrelevant

**Q5. From where do you get ideas about how to improve the performance of your local authority?**
a. National associations of local authorities (for example International City/County Management Association)
b. Consultants
c. The federal government
d. The state
e. The media
f. International organizations (for example the OECD)
g. Other local authorities in your country (peer review)
h. Universities and colleges
i. Local authorities in other countries

For each of these items, response alternatives are:

1. Frequently
2. Sometimes
3. Never
4. Irrelevant

**Q6. How important would you say that the local political leadership (the Mayor) is for the city's economic development strategy, the types of services provided and for the local tax level?**
a. Local economic development strategy
b. Types of services provided
c. Local tax level

For each of these items, response alternatives are:

1. Very important
2. Somewhat important
3. Not important
4. Irrelevant

**Q7. How would you describe changes in the relationships between the central, prefectural and local levels of government during the past several years?**
a. There has been a transfer of authority from the federal government to local governments
b. There has been a transfer of authority from the federal government to the states
c. There has been a transfer of authority from the states to local governments
d. The city has had to take an increasing financial responsibility for delivering federal programs
e. Federal subsidies to local authorities have been merged into fewer subsidies
f. The city's dependence on federal and state government for financial support has increased
g. There is less political control by the federal government over local authorities today

For each of these items, response alternatives are:

1. Agree strongly
2. Agree somewhat
3. Disagree somewhat
4. Disagree strongly
5. Irrelevant

**Q8. Has the city been part of efforts to strengthen the state?**
Response alternatives:

1. Yes, within the metropolitan region which the city is part of
2. Yes, within the rural region which the city is part of
3. The city has chosen not to participate in such state projects
4. No such efforts have been launched

**Q9. Overall, would you say that the state level is becoming more or less important in terms of coordination and economic development?**
For each of (a) coordination and (b) economic development, response alternatives:

1. Much more important
2. Somewhat more important
3. Less important
4. Much less important

# References

Albert, M. (1993), *Capitalism Against Capitalism* (London: Whurr).

Aldecoa, F. and M. Keating (eds) (1999), *Paradiplomacy in Action: The Foreign Relations of Subnational Governments* (London: Frank Cass).

Alger, C.F. (1998), "Perceiving, Analyzing and Coping with the Local–Global Nexus", *International Social Science Journal* 117:340–41.

Alger, C.F. (2010), "Expanding Governmental Diversity in Global Governance: Parliamentarians of State and Local Governments", *Global Governance* 16:59–79.

Allison, G.T. (1986), "Public and Private Management: Are they Fundamentally Alike in all Unimportant Respects?", in F.W. Lane (ed.), *Current Issues in Public Administration* (New York, NY: St. Martin's), 184–200.

Altman, R.C. (2009a), "The Great Crash, 2008: A geopolitical setback for the West", *Foreign Affairs* (January/February), 1–7.

Altman, R.C. (2009b), "Globalization in Retreat: Further Geopolitical Consequences of the Financial Crisis", *Foreign Affairs* (July/August), 1–6.

Amoore, L., R. Dodgson, B.K. Gillis, L. Langley and D. Marshall (1997), "Overturning 'Globalisation': Resisting the Teleological, Reclaiming the Political", *New Political Economy* 2:179–95.

Amyx, J.A. (2004), *Japan's Financial Crisis: Institutional Rigidity and Reluctant Change* (Princeton, NJ: Princeton University Press).

Bache, I. and M. Flinders (eds) (2004), *Multi-level Governance* (Oxford: Oxford University Press).

Ban, C. (1998), "Reinventing the Federal Civil Service: Drivers of Change", *Public Administration Quarterly* 22:21–34.

Barnes, W.R. (2005), "Beyond Federal Urban Policy", *Urban Affairs Review* 40:575–89.

Basu Das, S. (ed.) (2012), *Achieving the ASEAN Economic Community*

*2015: Challenges for Member Countries and Businesses* (Singapore: Institute of Southeast Asian Studies).

Beauregard, R.A. (1995), "Theorizing the Global–Local Connection", in P.L. Knox and P.J. Taylor (eds), *World Cities in a World-System* (Cambridge: Cambridge University Press), 232–48.

Beauregard, R.A. and J. Pierre (2000), "Disputing the Global: A Sceptical View of Locality-Based International Initiatives", *Policy and Politics* 28:465–78.

Beeson, M. and A. Capling (2002), "Australia in the World Economy: Globalisation, International Institutions, and Economic Governance", in S. Bell (ed.), *Economic Governance and Institutional Dynamics* (Oxford: Oxford University Press), 285–303.

Bell, S. and A. Hindmoor (2009), *Rethinking Governance: The Centrality of the State in Modern Society* (Cambridge: Cambridge University Press).

Bennett, C.J. (1991), "Review Article: What Is Policy Convergence and What Causes It?", *British Journal of Political Science* 21:215–33.

Berger, S. (1996), "Introduction", in S. Berger and R. Dore (eds), *National Diversity and Global Capitalism* (Ithaca: Cornell University Press), 1–28.

Berger, S. and R. Dore (eds) (1996), *National Diversity and Global Capitalism* (Ithaca: Cornell University Press).

Betsill, M.M. and H. Buckeley (2004), "Transnational Networks and Global Environmental Governance: The Cities for Climate Protection Program", *International Studies Quarterly* 48:471–93.

Bilder, R.B. (1989), "The Role of States and Cities in International Relations", *American Journal of International Law* 83:421–31.

Blomqvist, P. (2004), "The Choice Revolution: Privatization of Swedish Welfare Services in the 1990s", *Social Policy and Administration* 38:139–55.

Blyth, M. (2008), "One Ring to Bind Them All: American Power and Neoliberal Capitalism", in J. Kopstein and S. Steinmo (eds), *Growing Apart? America and Europe in the Twenty-First Century* (Cambridge: Cambridge University Press), 109–35.

Boyer, R. (1996), "The Convergence Hypothesis Revisited: Globalization but Still the Century of Nations?", in S. Berger and R. Dore (eds), *National Diversity and Global Capitalism* (Ithaca: Cornell University Press), 29–59.

Boyer, R. and D. Drache (eds) (1996), *States Against Markets: The Limits of Globalization* (London: Routledge).

Brenner, N. (1999), "Globalisation as Reterritorialisation: The Re-scaling of Urban Governance in the European Union", *Urban Studies* 36:431–51.

Brenner, N. (2004), *New State Spaces: Urban Governance and the Rescaling of Statehood* (Oxford: Oxford University Press).

Brotchie, J., M. Beatty, E. Blakeley, P. Hall, and P. Newton (eds) (1995), *Cities in Competition* (Melbourne: Longman Australia).

Brudney, J.L., F.T. Hebert and D.S. Wright (1999), "Reinventing Government in the American States: Measuring and Explaining Administrative Reform", *Public Administration Review* 59:19–30.

Brunsson, N. (1989), *The Organization of Hypocrisy* (New York, NY: Wiley).

Brunsson, N. and B. Jacobsson (eds) (2000), *A World of Standards* (Oxford: Oxford University Press).

Brunsson, N. and J.P. Olsen (1993), *The Reforming Organization* (London: Routledge).

Buck, N., I. Gordon, A. Harding and I. Turok (eds) (2005), *Changing Cities: Rethinking Urban Competitiveness, Cohesion and Governance* (Basingstoke: Palgrave).

Cameron, M.A. and B.W. Tomlin (2000), *The Making of NAFTA: How the Deal was Done* (Ithaca: Cornell University Press).

Camilleri, J.A. and J. Falk (1992), *The End of Sovereignty* (Aldershot, UK and Brookfield, VT, USA: Edward Elgar Publishing).

Campbell, J., J.R. Hollingsworth and L.N. Lindberg (eds) (1991), *Governance of the American Economy* (Cambridge: Cambridge University Press).

Cerny, P.G. (1990), *The Changing Architecture of Politics: Structure, Agency, and the Future of the State* (London: Sage).

Cerny, P.G. (2005), "Governance, Globalization and the Japanese Financial System: Resistance or Restructuring?", in G.D. Hook (ed.), *Contested Governance in Japan: Sites and issues* (London: Routledge), 90–110.

Christensen, T. and P. Laegreid (eds) (2011), *The Ashgate Research Companion to New Public Management* (Farnham: Ashgate).

Clarke, S.E. (2003), "Globalism and Cities: A North American Perspective", in R. Hambleton, H.V. Savitch and M. Stewart (eds), *Globalism and Local Democracy: Challenge and Change in Europe and North America* (Basingstoke: Palgrave), 30–51.

Clarke, S.E. (2006), "Globalisation and the Study of Local Politics: Is the Study of Local Politics Meaningful in the Global Age?", in H. Baldersheim and H. Wollmann (eds), *The Comparative Study of Local Government and Politics: Overview and Synthesis* (Leverkusen: Barbara Budrich Publishers), 33–65.

Colignon, R.A. (2003), *Amakudari: The Hidden Fabric of Japan's Economy* (Ithaca: Cornell University Press).

Dennis, B. (1998), *500 %* (Stockholm: DN:s Förlag).

Dollery, B.E., J. Garcia and E.C. Lesage, Jr. (2008), "Introduction", in B.E. Dollery, J. Garcia and E.C. Lesage, Jr. (eds), *Local Government Reform: A Comparative Analysis of Advanced Anglo-American Democracies* (Cheltenham, UK and Northampton, MA, USA: Edward Elgar Publishing), 1–15.

Douglass, M. (1988), "The Transnationalization of Urbanization in Japan", *International Journal of Urban and Regional Research* 12:425–54.

Drezner, D.W. (2001), "Globalization and Policy Convergence", *International Studies Review* 3:53–78.

Eckes, Jr., A.E. and T.W. Zeiler (2003), *Globalization and the American Century* (Cambridge: Cambridge University Press).

Eisinger, P.K. (1989), *The Rise of the Entrepreneurial State: State and Local Economic Development Policy in the United States* (Madison: The University of Wisconsin Press).

Eisner, M.A. (2000), *Regulatory Politics in Transition* (2nd edn) (Baltimore: Johns Hopkins University Press).

Elder, M. (2003), "METI and Industrial Policy in Japan: Change and Continuity", in U. Schaede and W. Grimes (eds), *Japan's Managed Globalization: Adapting to the Twenty-First Century* (Armonk, N.Y: M. E. Sharpe), 159–90.

Englund, P. (1999), "The Swedish Banking Crisis: Roots and Consequences", *Oxford Review of Economic Policy* 15:80–97.

Evans, P. (1997), "The Eclipse of the State? Reflections on Stateness in an Era of Globalization", *World Politics* 50:62–87.

Evans, P. (1998), "What Future for the State in a Global Political Economy?", *Swiss Political Science Review* 4:107–16.

Evans, P. (2005), "Between Regionalism and Regionalization: Policy Networks and the Nascent East Asian Institutional Identity", in T.J. Pempel (ed.), *Reshaping East Asia: The Construction of a Region* (Ithaca: Cornell University Press), 195–215.

Feiock, R.C. (ed.) (2004), *Metropolitan Governance: Conflict,*

*Competition, and Cooperation* (Washington, DC: Georgetown University Press).

Feldstein, M. (1998), "Refocusing the IMF", *Foreign Affairs* 77:20–33.

Frenkel, R. (2003), "Globalization and Financial Crises in Latin America", *Cepal Review* 80:39–51.

Fry, E.H. (1998), *The Expanding Role of State and Local Governments in U. S. Foreign Policy Affairs* (New York, NY: Council on Foreign Relations Press).

Fry, E.H. (2013), "Cities confront Globalization: Municipal Foreign Affairs and other Coping Devices", in P.K. Kresl and J. Sobrino (eds), *Handbook on Research Methods And Applications in Urban Economies* (Cheltenham, UK and Northampton, MA, USA: Edward Elgar Publishing).

Fry, E.H., L.H. Radebaugh and P. Soldatos (eds) (1989), *The New International Cities Era: The Global Activities of North American Municipal Governments* (Provo, UH: David M. Kennedy for International Studies, Brigham Young University).

Gamble, A. (1994), *Britain in Decline* (4th edn) (Basingstoke: Macmillan).

Garrett, G. (1995), "Capital Mobility, Trade, and the Domestic Politics of Economic Policy", *International Organization* 49:657–87.

Garrett, G. (2000), "The Causes of Globalization", *Comparative Political Studies* 33:941–91.

Garrett, G. and D. Mitchell (2001), "Globalization, Government Spending and Taxation in the OECD", *European Journal of Political Research* 39:145–77.

Genschel, P. (2004), "Globalization and the Welfare State: A Retrospective", *Journal of European Public Policy* 11:613–36.

Glatzer, M. and D. Rueschemeyer (eds) (2005), *Globalization and the Future of the Welfare State* (Pittsburgh: University of Pittsburgh Press).

Goetz, E.G. and S.E. Clarke (eds) (1993), *The New Localism: Comparative Urban Politics in a Global Era* (Newbury Park: Sage).

Goldfinch, S. and P. t' Hart (2003), "Leadership and Institutional Reform: Engineering Macroeconomic Policy Change in Australia", *Governance: An International Journal of Policy, Administration, and Institutions* 16:235–70.

Goldsmith, M. (1993), "The Europeanisation of Local Government", *Urban Studies* 30:683–99.
Graham, O.L. (1992), *Losing Time: The Industrial Policy Debate* (Cambridge, MA: Harvard University Press).
Gustafsson, L. and A. Svensson (1999), *Public Sector Reform in Sweden* (Malmö: Liber).
Haas, P. (1992), "Introduction: Epistemic Communities and International Policy Coordination", *International Organization* 46:1–35.
Hall, P.A. (1986), *Governing the Economy: The Politics of State Intervention in Britain and France* (Oxford: Oxford University Press).
Hall, P.A. and D. Soskice (eds) (2001), *Varieties of Capitalism: The Institutional Foundations of Comparative Advantage* (Oxford: Oxford University Press).
Hambleton, R. and J. Simone Gross (eds) (2007), *Governing Cities in a Global Era* (Basingstoke: Palgrave).
Hamilton, A., J. Madison and J. Jay (1961), *The Federalist Papers* (New York, NY: New American Library).
Hay, C. and B. Rosamond (2002), "Globalization, European Integration and the discursive construction of economic imperatives", *Journal of European Public Policy* 9:147–67.
Helleiner, E. (1994), *States and the Reemergence of Global Finance* (Ithaca: Cornell University Press).
Henning, R. (1987), *Näringspolitik i obalans* [Industrial policy out of balance] (Stockholm: Allmänna Förlaget).
Hill, R.C. and K. Fujita (1995), "Osaka's Tokyo Problem", *International Journal of Urban and Regional Research* 19:181–93.
Hinnfors, J. and J. Pierre (1998), "The Politics of Currency Crises in Sweden: Domestic Policy Choice in a Globalized Economy", *West European Politics* 21:103–19.
Hirst, P. and G. Thompson (1999), *Globalization in Question: The International Economy and the Possibilities of Governance* (Oxford: Polity Press).
Hobbs, H.H. (1994), *City Hall Goes Abroad: The Foreign Policy of Local Politics* (Thousand Oaks, CA: Sage).
Hoekman, B. and M. Kostecki (1995), *The Political Economy of the World Trading System* (Oxford: Oxford University Press).
Hood, C. (1991). A Public Management for all Seasons? *Public Administration*, 69:3–19.

Hood, C. (1995), "'Deprivileging' the UK civil service in the 1980s: Dream or reality?", in J. Pierre (ed.), *Bureaucracy and the Modern State: An Introduction to Comparative Public Administration* (Aldershot, UK and Brookfield, VT, USA: Edward Elgar Publishing), 92–117.

Hooghe, L. and G. Marks (2003), "Unraveling the State, but How? Types of Multi-level Governance", *American Political Science Review* 97:233–43.

Hook, G.D. (2001), "Japan's role in the East Asian political economy: an emerging region?", in G.D. Hook and H. Harukiyo (eds), *The Political Economy of Japanese Globalization* (London: Routledge), 40–55.

Hoshino, S. (1996), "Japanese Local Government in an Era of Global Economic Interdependency", in J.S. Jung and D.S. Wright (eds), *Globalization and Decentralization: Institutional Contexts, Policy Issues, and Intergovernmental Relations in Japan and the United States* (Washington, DC: Georgetown University Press), 359–73.

Hufbauer, G.C. and J.J. Schott (1993), *NAFTA: An Assessment* (revised edition) (Washington, DC: Institute for International Economics).

Hytrek, G. and K.M. Zentgraf (2008), *America Transformed: Globalization, Inequality, and Power* (Oxford: Oxford University Press).

Ikenberry, G.J. (2007), "Globalization as American Hegemony", in D. Held and A.G. McGrew (eds) (2007), *Globalization Theory: Approaches and Controversies* (Cambridge: Polity Press), 41–61.

Itoh, M. (1995), "Administrative Reform", in Hyung-Ki Kim, M. Muramatsu, T.J. Pempel and K. Yamamura (eds), *The Japanese Civil Service and Economic Development: Catalysts of Change* (Oxford: Clarendon Press), 235–60.

Itoh, M. (1998), *Globalization of Japan: Japanese* Sakoku *Mentality and U.S. Efforts to Open Japan* (New York, NY: St. Martin's Press).

Jabbra, J.G. and O.P. Dwivedi (eds) (2005), *Administrative Culture in a Global Context* (Whitby, ON: de Sitter).

Jacobs, A.J. (2004), "Federations of Municipalities: A Practical Alternative to Local Government Consolidations in Japan?", *Governance: An International Journal of Policy, Administration, and Institutions* 17:247–74.

Jacobsson, B. and G. Sundström (2006), *Från Hemvävd till invävd: Europeiseringen av svensk förvaltning och politik* [From homegrown to embedded: The Europeanization of Swedish administration and politics] (Malmö: Liber).

Jayasuria, K. (2002), "Governance, Post-Washington Consensus and the New Anti-Politics", in T. Lindsey and H. Dick (eds), *Corruption in Asia: Rethinking the Governance Paradigm* (Sydney: The Federation Press), 24–36.

Jensen, L. (2003), *Den store koordinator: Finansministeriet som moderne styringsaktör* [The Great Coordinator: The Ministry of Finance as a modern governance actor] (Copenhagen: Jurist- og Ökonomforbundets Forlag).

Jesuit, D.K. and L. Sych (2012), "Local Economic Development and Cross-Border Networks", *International Journal of Public Sector Management* 25:473–82.

Johansson, J. (1991), *Offentligt och privat i regionpolitiken* [Public and Private in Regional Policy] (Lund: Department of Political Science, University of Lund).

Johnson, C.A. (1982), *MITI and the Japanese Miracle* (Stanford, CA: Stanford University Press).

Johnson, C.A. (1998), "Economic Crisis in East Asia: The Clash of Capitalisms", *Cambridge Journal of Economics* 22:653–61.

Johnson, P.M. and A. Beaulieu (1996), *The Environment and NAFTA: Understanding and Implementing the New Continental Law* (Washington, DC: Island Press).

Kahler, M. and D.A. Lake (eds) (2003a), *Governance in a Global Economy: Political Authority in Transition* (Princeton, NJ: Princeton University Press).

Kahler, M. and D.A. Lake (eds) (2003b), "Globalization and Governance", in M. Kahler and D.A. Lake (eds), *Governance in a Global Economy: Political Authority in Transition* (Princeton, NJ: Princeton University Press), 1–32.

Kamo, T. (2000), "An Aftermath of Globalisation? East Asian Economic Turmoil and Japanese Cities Adrift", *Urban Studies* 37:2146–65.

Kaplan, J. and F. James (eds) (1990), *The Future of National Urban Policy* (Durham: Duke University Press).

Katz, B.J. (ed.) (2000), *Reflections on Regionalism* (Washington, DC: The Brookings Institution).

Katzenstein, P.J. (1984), *Corporatism and Change: Austria,*

*Switzerland and the Politics of Industry* (Ithaca: Cornell University Press).
Katzenstein, P.J. (1985), *Small States in World Markets: Industrial Policy in Europe* (Ithaca: Cornell University Press).
Katzenstein, P.J. (2005), *A World of Regions: Asia and Europe in the American Imperium* (Ithaca: Cornell University Press).
Keating, M. (1991), *Comparative Urban Politics* (Aldershot, UK and Brookfield, VT, USA: Edward Elgar Publishing).
*Keidanren Review*, 1995 (May).
Keil, R. (1998), "Globalization Makes States: Perspectives on Local Governance in the Age of the World City", *Review of International Political Economy* 5:616–46.
Kenworthy, L. (1995), *In Search of National Economic Success: Balancing Competition and Cooperation* (Thousand Oaks, CA: Sage).
Keohane, R.O. and H.W. Milner (1996), *Internationalization and Domestic Politics* (Cambridge: Cambridge University Press).
Kester, W.K. (1996), "American and Japanese Corporate Governance: Convergence to Best Practice?", in S. Berger and R. Dore (eds), *National Diversity and Global Capitalism* (Ithaca: Cornell University Press), 107–37.
Kettl, D.F. (1994), *Reinventing Government? Appraising the National Performance Review* (Washington, DC: The Brookings Institution).
Kettl, D.F. (1997), "The Global Revolution in Public Management: Driving Themes, Missing Links", *Journal of Policy Analysis and Management* 16:446–62.
Kettl, D.F. (2002), *The Transformation of Governance: Public Administration for the Twenty-First Century America* (Baltimore: Johns Hopkins University Press).
Kim, D. and S. Kim (2003), "Globalization, Financial Crisis, and Industrial Relations: The Case of South Korea", *Industrial Relations: A Journal of Economy and Society* 42:341–67.
King, D.S. and J. Pierre (eds) (1990), *Challenges to Local Government* (London: Sage).
Knox, P.L. and P.J. Taylor (eds) (1995), *World Cities in a World-System* (Cambridge: Cambridge University Press).
KOF Swiss Economic Institute (2013), "KOF Index of Globalization 2013: Slight Recovery of Economic Globalization".
Korpi, W. (2003), "Welfare-State Regress in Western Europe:

Politics, Institution, Globalization, and Europeanization", *Annual Review of Sociology* 29:589–609.

Kosai, Y. (1996), "Competition and Competition Policy in Japan: Foreign Pressures and Domestic Institutions", in S. Berger and R. Dore (eds), *National Diversity and Global Capitalism* (Ithaca: Cornell University Press), 197–215.

Krantz, O. (2008), "Economic Growth and Economic Policy in Sweden in the 20th century: A Comparative Perspective", in M. Müller and T. Myllyntaus (eds), *Pathbreakers: Small European Countries Responding to Globalisation and Deglobalisation* (Bern: Peter Lang), 39–64.

Krauss, E.S. and T.J. Pempel (eds) (2004), *Beyond Bilateralism: U.S.–Japan Relationships in the New Asia-Pacific* (Stanford, CA: Stanford University Press).

Krauss, E.S. and J. Pierre (1990), "The Decline of Dominant Parties: Parliamentary Politics in Japan and Sweden During the 1970s", in T.J. Pempel (ed.), *Uncommon Democracies: The One-Party Dominant Regimes* (Ithaca: Cornell University Press), 226–59.

Kresl, P.K. and E.H. Fry (2005), *An Urban Response to Internationalization* (Cheltenham, UK and Northampton, MA, USA: Edward Elgar Publishing).

Krugman, P. (1994a), *Peddling Prosperity* (New York, NY: W.W. Norton & Co).

Krugman, P. (1994b), *Currencies and Crises* (Cambridge, MA: MIT Press).

Kudo, A. (2001), "Americanization or Europeanization? The Globalization of the Japanese Economy", in G.D. Hook and H. Harukiyo (eds), *The Political Economy of Japanese Globalization* (London: Routledge), 120–36.

Kudo, A. (2006), "The Response of Japanese Capitalism to Globalization: A Comparison with the German Case", in G.D. Hook and H. Hasegawa (eds), *Japanese Responses to Globalization: Politics, Security, Economics and Business* (Basingstoke: Palgrave), 131–50.

Kuczynski, P-P. (2003), "Setting the Stage", in P-P. Kuczynski and J. Williams (eds), *After the Washington Consensus: Restarting Growth and Reform in Latin America* (Washington, DC: Institute for International Economics), 21–32.

Leftwich, A. (1994), "Governance, the State and the Politics of Development", *Development and Change* 25:363–86.

Le Galès, P. and C. Lequesne (eds) (1998), *Regions in Europe* (London: Routledge).

Lidström, A. (2011), "Local Government Associations in the World: A Research Proposal" (paper presented at the annual meeting of the Swedish Political Science Association, Umeå University, October 27–28).

Light, P. (1997), *The Tides of Reform: Making Government Work, 1945–1995* (New Haven, CT: Yale University Press).

Lindbeck, A. (1998), *Det svenska experimentet* [The Swedish Experiment] (Stockholm: SNS).

Lundgren, B. (1998), *När bubblan brast: Om den svåraste finanskrisen i Sveriges historia* [When the Bubble Burst: The Biggest Financial Crisis in Swedish History] (Stockholm: Bokförlaget DN).

Lundqvist, L.J. (1998), "Local-to-local Partnerships among Swedish Municipalities: Why and How Neighbours Join to Alleviate Resource Constraints", in J. Pierre (ed.), *Partnerships in Urban Governance. European and American Experiences* (Basingstoke: Palgrave), 93–111.

Lundqvist, L.J. (2012), "Environmental Policy Convergence through Ecological Modernization" (paper presented at the Annual Conference of the Swedish political Science Association, September 26–28).

Lynn, L.E. Jr. (2001), "Globalization and Administrative Reform: What is Happening in Theory?", *Public Management Review* 3:191–208.

Madrick, J. (2009), *The Case for Big Government* (Princeton, NJ: Princeton University Press).

Mann, M. (1997), "Has Globalization ended the Rise and Rise of the Nation-State?", *Review of International Political Economy*, 4:472–96.

Manning, N. (2001), "The Legacy of the New Public Management in Developing Countries", *International Journal of Administrative Sciences* 67:296–310.

March, J.G. and J.P. Olsen (1989), *Rediscovering Institutions: The Organizational Basis of Politics* (New York: Free Press).

Marcuse, P. and R. van Kempen (2000), "Conclusion: A Changed Spatial Order", in P. Marcuse and R. van Kempen (eds), *Globalizing Cities: A New Spatial Order?* (Oxford: Blackwell), 249–75.

Marks, G., L. Hooghe and K. Blank (1996), "European Integration

since the 1980s: State-centric vs. Multi-level Governance", *Journal of Common Market Studies* 34:341–78.
Massey, D.B. (1995), *Spatial Divisions of Labor: Social Structures and the Geography of Production* (2nd edn) (New York, NY: Routledge).
Masujima, T. (2005), "Administrative Reform in Japan: Past Development and Future Trends", *International Review of Administrative Sciences* 71:295–308.
Miller, P. and N.S. Rose (2008), *Governing the Present: Administering Economic, Social and Personal Life* (Cambridge: Polity Press).
Moore, M.H. (1995), *Creating Public Value: Strategic Management in Government* (Cambridge, MA: Harvard University Press).
Mosley, L. (2003), *Global Capital and National Governments* (Cambridge: Cambridge University Press).
Muramatsu, M. (1997), *Local Power in the Japanese State* (Berkeley, CA: University of California Press).
Muramatsu, M. and J. Matsunami (2003), "The Late and Sudden Emergence of New Public Management Reforms in Japan", in H. Wollmann (ed.), *Evaluation in Public-Sector Reform: Concepts and Practice in International Perspective* (Cheltenham, UK and Northampton, MA, USA: Edward Elgar Publishing), 169–81.
Mörth, U. (ed.) (2004), *Soft Law in Governance and Regulation: An Interdisciplinary Analysis* (Cheltenham, UK and Northampton, MA, USA: Edward Elgar Publishing).
Nakamura, A. (1996), "Administrative Reform and Decentralization of Central Power: A Cross-national Comparison with Japan", *Asian Review of Public Administration* 8:4–13.
Nederveen Pieterse, J. (2004), *Globalization or Empire?* (London: Routledge).
Nester, W.R. (1997), *American Industrial Policy: Free or Managed Markets?* (New York, NY: St. Martin's Press).
Newman, P. (2000), "Changing Patterns of Regional Governance in the EU", *Urban Studies* 37: 895–908.
Niklasson, B. and J. Pierre (2012), "Does Agency Age Matter in Administrative Reform? Policy Autonomy and Public Management in Swedish Agencies", *Policy and Society* 31:195–210.
Nilsson, L. (ed.) (2010), En Region Blir Till [A Region is Born] (Gothenburg: The SOM Institute).
Norris, P. and R. Inglehart (2009), *Cosmopolitan Communications:*

*Cultural Diversity in a Globalized World* (New York, NY: Cambridge University Press).

North, D.C. (1990), *Institutions, Institutional Change and Economic Performance* (Cambridge: Cambridge University Press).

Nye, J.R. (2003), *The Paradox of American Power: Why the World's Only Superpower Can't Go It Alone* (Oxford: Oxford University Press).

Öberg, P. (1994), *Särintresse och Allmänintresse: Korporatismens ansikten* [Particular and public interest: The Faces of Corporatism] (Stockholm: Almqvist & Wiksell International).

OECD (2005), *Trade and Structural Adjustment* (Paris: OECD).

Ohmae, K. (1995), *The End of the Nation State: The Rise of Regional Economics* (London: Harper Collins).

Okimoto, D.I. (1988), *Between MITI and the Market* (Stanford, CA: Stanford University Press).

Olsen, J.P. (1996), "Slow Learner—or Another Triumph of the Tortoise?", in B.G. Peters and J.P. Olsen (eds), *Lessons from Experience: Experiential Learning in Administrative Reforms in Eight Democracies* (Oslo: Scandinavian University Press), 180–213.

Olsen, J.P. (2010), *Governing through Institution Building: Institutional Theory and Recent European Experiments in Democratic Organization* (Oxford: Oxford University Press).

Olson, M. (1984), *The Rise and Decline of Nations: Economic Growth, Stagflation, and Social Rigidities* (New Haven, CT: Yale University Press).

Osborne, D. and T. Gaebler (1992), *Reinventing Government: How the Entrepreneurial Spirit is Transforming the Public Sector* (Reading, MA: Addison-Wesley).

Pain, N. and I. Koske (2007), "The Effects of Globalisation on Labour Markets, Productivity and Inflation" (Paris: OECD).

Painter, M. and B.G. Peters (eds) (2010), *Tradition and Public Administration* (Basingstoke: Palgrave).

Parkinson, M. and D. Judd (1988), "Urban Revitalization in America and the U.K: The Politics of Uneven Development", in M. Parkinson, B. Foley, and D. Judd (eds), *Regenerating the Cities: The UK Crisis and the US Experience* (Manchester: Manchester University Press), 1–8.

Pastor, M., T.W. Lester and J. Scoggins (2009), "Why Regions? Why Now? Who Cares?", *Journal of Urban Affairs* 31:269–96.

Pempel, T.J. (ed.) (2005), *Reshaping East Asia: The Construction of a Region* (Ithaca: Cornell University Press).

Pempel, T.J. and M. Muramatsu (1995), "The Japanese Bureaucracy and Economic Development", in H-K. Kim, M. Muramatsu, T.J. Pempel and K. Yamamura (eds), *The Japanese Civil Service and Economic Development: Catalysts of Change* (Oxford: Clarendon Press), 19–76.

Pempel, T.J. and K. Tsunekawa (1979), "Corporatism without Labor?: The Japanese Anomaly", in P. Schmitter and G. Lehmbruch (eds), *Trends Towards Corporatist Intermediation* (Beverly Hills, CA: Sage), 231–70.

Perry, J., H.A.G.M. Bekke and T.A.J. Toonen (eds) (1996), *Civil Service Systems in Comparative Perspective* (Bloomington, IN: University of Indiana Press).

Peters, B.G. (2000), "Globalization, Institutions, and Governance", in B.G. Peters and D.J. Savoie (eds), *Governance in the Twenty-first Century* (Montreal and Kingston: McGill-Queen's University Press), 29–57.

Peters, B.G. (2001), *The Future of Governing* (2nd edn) (Lawrence, KS: University of Kansas Press).

Peters, B.G. (2013), *Strategies for Comparative Research in Political Science* (Basingstoke: Palgrave).

Peters, B.G. and J. Pierre (2007), "Governance and Civil Service Systems: From Easy Answers to Hard Questions", in J.C.N. Raadschelders, T.A.J. Toonen and F. van der Meer (eds), *The Civil Service in the 21st Century: Comparative Perspectives* (Basingstoke: Palgrave), 231–45.

Philippi, C. (2003), "Between 'Washington Consensus' and 'Asian Way': Japanese newspaper authors discussing the East Asian financial and economic crisis of 1997/1998", in *Japanstudien 15: Missverständnisse in der Begegnung mit Japan* (Munich: Iudicum Verlag), 281–314.

Piattoni, S. (2010), *The Theory of Multi-Level Governance: Conceptual, Empirical, and Normative Challenges* (Oxford: Oxford University Press).

Pierre, J. (1992), *Kommunerna, näringslivet och näringspolitiken: Sveriges lokala politiska ekonomier* [Municipalities, Businesses, and Economic Development Policy: Sweden's Local Political Economies] (Stockholm: SNS).

Pierre, J. (1993), "Legitimacy, Institutional Change, and the Politics of Public Administration in Sweden", *International Political Science Review*, 14:387–401.

Pierre, J. (1995), "Comparative Public Administration: the State of the Art", in J. Pierre (ed.), *Bureaucracy in the Modern State: An Introduction to Comparative Public Administration* (Aldershot, UK and Brookfield, VT, USA: Edward Elgar Publishing), 1–17.

Pierre, J. (1999), *Marknaden som Politisk Aktör: Politik och Finansmarknad i 1990-talets Sverige* [Markets as Political Actors: Politics and Financial Markets in Sweden in the 1990s] (Stockholm: Royal Commission on the state of democracy in Sweden, SOU1999:131, vol. 11).

Pierre, J. (2011a), "Stealth Economy?: Economic Theory and the Politics of Administrative Reform", *Administration and Society* 43:672–92.

Pierre, J. (2011b), *The Politics of Urban Governance* (Basingstoke: Palgrave).

Pierre, J. and S-C. Park (1997), "The Dynamics of Abstract and Manifest Institutional Change: MITI and the Japanese 'Economic Miracle' Reconsidered", *Governance: An International Journal of Policy, Administration, and Institutions* 10:351–76.

Pierre, J. and B.G. Peters (2000), *Governance, Politics and the State* (Basingstoke: Palgrave).

Pierson, P. (1994), *Dismantling the Welfare State?: Reagan, Thatcher and the Politics of Retrenchment* (Cambridge: Cambridge University Press).

Pilling, D. (2008), "A glimpse of a new shade of grey in Japan", *Financial Times*, September 4.

Pollitt, C. (2001), "Convergence: The Useful Myth?", *Public Administration* 79:933–47.

Pollitt, C. (2002), "Clarifying Convergence: Striking Similarities and Durable Differences in Public Management Reform", *Public Management Review* 4:471–92.

Pollitt, C. and G. Bouckaert (2011), *Public Management Reform: A Comparative Analysis* (3rd edn) (Oxford: Oxford University Press).

Porter, M.J. (1990), *The Competitive Advantage of Nations* (New York, NY: Free Press).

Przeworski, A. (1987), "Methods of Cross-National Research, 1970–1983: An Overview", in M. Dierkes et al. (eds), *Comparative*

*Policy Research: Learning from Experience* (Aldershot: Gower), 31–49.

Reinhart, C.M. and K.S. Rogoff (2008), *This Time is Different: A Panoramic View of Eight Centuries of Financial Folly* (Princeton, NJ: Princeton University Press).

Ruggie, J. (1998), "Globalization and the Embedded Liberalism Compromise: The End of an Era?", in W. Streek (ed.), *Internationale Wirtschaft, Nationale Demokratie: Herausforderungen för die Demokratietheorie* (Frankfurt am Main: Campus), 79–98.

Sassen, S. (1991), *The Global City: New York, London, Tokyo* (Princeton, NJ: Princeton University Press).

Sassen, S. (1996), "Cities and Communities in the Global Economy: Rethinking Our Concepts", *American Behavioral Scientist* 39:629–39.

Sassen, S. (2000), "The Global City: Strategic Site/New frontier", *American Studies* 41:79–95.

Savoie, D. (1994), *Thatcher, Reagan, Mulroney: In Search of a New Bureaucracy* (Pittsburgh, PA: Pittsburgh University Press).

Schaede, U. and W.W. Grimes (2003a), "Preface", in U. Schaede and W.W. Grimes (eds), *Japan's Managed Globalization: Adapting to the Twenty-First Century* (Armonk, NY: M.E. Sharpe), xi–xiii.

Schaede, U. and W.W. Grimes (2003b), "Introduction: The Emergence of Permeable Insulation", in U. Schaede and W.W. Grimes (eds), *Japan's Managed Globalization: Adapting to the Twenty-First Century* (Armonk, NY: M.E. Sharpe), 3–16.

Scharpf, F.W. (1994), "Games Real Actors Could Play: Positive and Negative Coordination in Embedded Negotiations", *Journal of Theoretical Politics* 6:27–53.

Scharpf, F.W. (1998), "Globalization: The Limitations on State Capacity", *Swiss Political Science Review* 4:92–8.

Schick, A. (1998), "Why Most Developing Countries Should Not Try New Zealand Reforms", *The World Bank Research Observer* 13:123–31.

Schmidt, V. (1999), "Convergent pressures, divergent responses: France, Great Britain and Germany between Globalization and Europeanization", in D.A. Smith, D.J. Solinger and S.C. Topik (eds), *States and Sovereignty in the Global Economy* (London: Routledge), 172–92.

Schwab, K. (2012), *The Global Competitiveness Report 2012–2013* (Geneva: World Economic Forum).

Schön, D.A. (1983), *The Reflective Practitioner: How Professionals Think in Action* (New York, NY: Basic Books).
Sellers, J.M. (2001), *Governing from Below: Urban Regions and the Global Economy* (Cambridge: Cambridge University Press).
Serra, N. and J.E. Stiglitz (eds) (2008), *The Washington Consensus Reconsidered: Towards a New Global Governance* (Oxford: Oxford University Press).
Shaw, M. (1997), "The State of Globalization: Toward a Theory of State Transformation", *Review of International Political Economy*, 4:497–513.
Smyrl, M.E. (1997), "Does European Community Regional Policy Empower the Regions?", *Governance*, 10:287–309.
Soeya, Y., M. Tadokoro, and D.A. Welch (2011), *Japan as a "Normal Country"? A Nation in Search of Its Place in the World* (Toronto: University of Toronto Press).
Sölvell, O. and M.E. Porter (1993), *Advantage Sweden* (2nd edn) (Basingstoke: Palgrave).
Sörensen, G. (2004), *The Transformation of the State: Beyond the Myth of Retreat* (Basingstoke: Palgrave).
Spulber, N. (1995), *The American Economy: The Struggle for Supremacy in the 21st Century* (Cambridge: Cambridge University Press).
Steinmo, S. (2012), *The Evolution of Modern States: Sweden, Japan, and the United States* (Cambridge: Cambridge University Press).
Steinmo, S., K. Thelen and F. Longstreth (eds) (1992), *Structuring Politics: Historical Institutionalism in Comparative Analysis* (Cambridge: Cambridge University Press).
Stiglitz, J.E. (2003), *Globalization and its Discontents* (New York, NY: W.W. Norton).
Storper, M. and R. Walker (1989), *The Capitalist Imperative: Territory, Technology, and Industrial Growth* (Oxford: Basil Blackwell).
Strange, S. (1996), *The Retreat of the State: The Diffusion of Power in the World Economy* (Cambridge: Cambridge University Press).
Stronach, B. (1995), *Beyond the Rising Sun: Nationalism in Contemporary Japan* (Westport, CT: Praeger).
Strömberg, L. and J. Westerståhl (eds) (1983), *De nya kommunerna* [The New Municipalities] (Stockholm: Liber).
Suleiman, E. (2003), *Dismantling Democratic States* (Princeton, NJ: Princeton University Press).

Summers, L.H. (1998), "American Farmers: Their Stake in Asia" (Office of Public Affairs, US Treasury Department, Washington, DC, February 23).

Sundström, G. (2003), *Stat på villovägar: Resultatstyrningens framväxt ur ett historiskt-institutionellt perspektiv* [The Wayward State: The Development of Management by Results in a Historical Institutional Perspective] (Stockholm: Stockholm Studies of Politics 96. Department of Political Science, University of Stockholm).

Svara, J. and C. Hoene (2008), "Local Government Reforms in the United States", in B.E. Dollery, J. Garcia, and E.C. LeSage, Jr. (eds), *Local Government Reform: A Comparative Analysis of Advanced Anglo-American Democracies* (Cheltenham, UK and Northampton, MA, USA: Edward Elgar Publishing), 133–57.

Sveriges Kommuner och Landsting (2008), "Medlemmarnas internationella engagemang" [The members' international involvement] (mimeo. Stockholm: Swedish Association of Local and Regional Authorities).

Swank, D. (2002), *Global Capital, Political Institutions, and Policy Change in Developed Welfare States* (Cambridge: Cambridge University Press).

Telasuo, C. (2000), *Småstater under internationalisering: Valutamarknadens avreglering i Sverige och Finland på 1980-talet. En studie i institutionell omvandling* [Small States Under Internationalisation: Deregulation of the Foreign Exchange Markets in Sweden and Finland during the 1980s. A Study of Institutional Change] (Department of Economic History, University of Gothenburg).

*The Economist* (2013), "Northern Lights: Special report on the Nordic Countries", February 2–8.

Thompson, J.R. (2000), "Reinvention as Reform: Assessing the National Performance Review", *Public Administration Review* 60:508–21.

Tiebout, C.M. (1956), "A Pure Theory of Local Expenditures", *Journal of Political Economy* 64:416–24.

Tillväxtverket (2012), "Företagens villkor och verklighet" [The Conditions and Realities of Private Businesses] (Stockholm: Tillväxtverket [The Swedish Agency for Economic and Regional Growth]).

Toonen, T.A.J. (2001), "The Comparative Dimension of

Administrative Reform: Creating Open Villages and Redesigning the Politics of Administration", in B.G. Peters and J. Pierre (eds), *Politicians, Bureaucrats and Administrative Reform* (London: Routledge), 183–201.

Turner, M. (2002), "Choosing Items from the Menu: New Public Management in Southeast Asia", *International Journal of Public Administration* 25:1493–1512.

Umegaki, M. (1988), *After the Restoration: The Beginning of Japan's Modern State* (New York, NY: New York University Press).

US National Performance Review (1993), *Creating a Government that Works Better and Costs Less: The Report of the National Performance Review* (Washington, DC: Government Printing Office).

van der Heiden, N. (2010), *Urban Foreign Policy and Domestic Dilemmas* (Colchester: ECPR Press).

Ventriss, C. (2000), "New Public Management: An Examination of Its Influence on Contemporary Public Affairs and its Impact on Shaping the Intellectual Agenda of the Field", *Administrative Theory & Praxis* 22:3, 500–518.

Vinh, S. (2004), "Ryotaro Shiba (1932–1996) and the Call for Meiji Values in a Global Age", in M. Nakamura (ed.), *Changing Japanese Business, Economy and Society: Globalization of Post-Bubble Japan* (Basingstoke: Palgrave), 17–39.

Wade, R. (1996), "Globalization and Its Limits: Reports of the Death of the National Economy are Greatly Exaggerated", in S. Berger and R. Dore (eds), *National Diversity and Global Capitalism* (Ithaca: Cornell University Press), 60–88.

Warren, R. (1990), "National Urban Policy and the Local State: Paradoxes of Meaning, Action and Consequences", *Urban Affairs Quarterly* 25:541–62.

Weaver, R.K. (1985), *The Politics of Industrial Change: Railway Policy in North America* (Washington, DC: Brookings Institution).

Weaver, R.K. and B.A. Rockman (eds) (1993), *Do Institutions Matter? Government Capabilities in the United States and Abroad* (Washington, DC: The Brookings Institution).

Weiss, L. (1998), *The Myth of the Powerless State* (Cambridge: Cambridge University Press).

Weiss, L. (1999), "Globalization and national governance: antimony or interdependence?", *Review of International Studies* 25:59–88.

Weiss, L. (2000), "Globalization and State Power", *Development and Society* 29:1–15.

Westney, D.E. (1987), *Imitation and Innovation: The Transfer of Western Organizational Patterns to Meiji Japan* (Cambridge: Cambridge University Press).

Wolf, M. (2008), "Financial Crisis Tests Durability of Globalisation", *Financial Times*, October 9.

Woo-Cumings, M. (1995), "Developmental Bureaucracy in Comparative Perspective: The Evolution of the Korean Civil Service", in H-G. Kim, M. Muramatsu, T.J. Pempel and K. Yamamura (eds), *The Japanese Civil Service and Economic Development* (New York, NY: Clarendon Press), 431–58.

Woo-Cumings, M. (2005), "Back to Basics: Ideology, Nationalism, and Asian Values in East Asia" in E. Helleiner and A. Prickel (eds), *Economic Nationalism in a Globalizing World* (Ithaca: Cornell University Press), 91–117.

Wright, D.S. and Y. Sakurai (1987), "Administrative Reform in Japan: Politics, Policy, and Public Administration in a Deliberative Society", *Public Administration Review* 47:121–33.

Yusoff, M.B., F.A. Hasan and S.A. Jalil (2000), *Globalisation, Economic Policy, and Equity: The Case of Malaysia* (Paris: OECD).

Zannakis, M. (2009), *Climate Policy as a Window of Opportunity: Sweden and Global Climate Change* (PhD dissertation) (Gothenburg: Department of Political Science, University of Gothenburg).

Zysman, J. (1983), *Governments, Markets, and Growth* (Ithaca and London: Cornell University Press).

# Index